UNTOLD

UNTOLD

A STORY OF LOVE, MOTHERHOOD, HEARTBREAK AND CHANGE

SNEŽANA WOOD

hachette
AUSTRALIA

hachette
AUSTRALIA

Published in Australia and New Zealand in 2024
by Hachette Australia
(an imprint of Hachette Australia Pty Limited)
Gadigal Country, Level 17, 207 Kent Street, Sydney, NSW 2000
www.hachette.com.au

Hachette Australia acknowledges and pays our respects to the past, present and future
Traditional Owners and Custodians of Country throughout Australia and recognises the
continuation of cultural, spiritual and educational practices of Aboriginal and Torres Strait Islander
peoples. Our head office is located on the lands of the Gadigal people of the Eora Nation.

A catalogue record for this
book is available from the
National Library of Australia

ISBN: 978 0 7336 4882 3 (paperback)

Cover design by Luke Causby, Blue Cork
Cover and chapter opener photography by Lauren Schulz Visuals
Top right photograph on page 166 by Vicky Papas; Vergara
Wedding photography on page 188 by Alice Mahran
All other images from the author's personal collection
Typeset in 12/20pt Sabon LT Std by Kirby Jones
Printed and bound in Great Britain by Clays Ltd, Elcograf S.p.A.

MIX
Paper | Supporting
responsible forestry
FSC® C104740

To my beautiful daughters.
May you always chase your dreams,
face your fears boldly, and remember that magic
lives beyond them.
This book is dedicated to you – boundless in
potential and possibility.

CONTENTS

1 On rolling with the punches   1

2 On freedom   27

3 On the devil you know   51

4 On rising from the ashes   67

5 On taking chances   89

6 On new normals   109

7 On trusting your gut   129

8 On the harshness of the spotlight   145

9 On strength   165

10 On marriage   187

11 On loss   203

12 On survival   217

13 On having a beautiful mind   241

14 On being in business   257

15 On finding balance (or not)   267

16 On caring less and loving more   283

CHAPTER 1

ON ROLLING WITH THE PUNCHES

My father named me Snežana. In Macedonian, the name translates to 'Snow White', which is a traditional and elegant name from this region. It comes from the Slavic word *sneg*, meaning snow. My name reflects the purity and beauty associated with snow in Macedonian culture, like winter's first snowfall, a name as individual, distinctive and unique as each snowflake. In Australia, however, my name is as rare as a snowman in the outback.

As a kid in Australia, land of 'G'day mate', my name stood out. Growing up, it was a daily challenge, a tongue twister for most. I became like a broken record, constantly repeating my name so many times that even I started questioning if I was saying it right. Nevertheless, I now love everything about my name. I've also found a solution, a much simpler way to help people with the pronunciation ... 'Sneshana', or the more iconic, 'Can you say parmigiana?'

I was born in Perth in 1980 to immigrant parents from North Macedonia. My dad, Marko, was born in Sirula, a village in the mountains, and as clichéd as it may sound, he walked through rough terrain for kilometres just to get to school. No car, no school bus, and if he was lucky he could sometimes hitch a ride on the family horse and cart, but these occurrences were few and far between. When he was thirteen, Dad emigrated to Perth with his family when his father got a job working on the railway lines in Tom Price, northern WA.

My mum, Menka, made a similar long trek to school from her village of Izdeglavje, although they didn't have a horse and cart, they had a bull and cart. She enjoyed being at school but when she was fifteen she had to leave to help her family with their crops and livestock, including bulls, cows, goats, sheep and chickens. Their water had to be collected from a well down the road and their toilets were outside. The only difference between their outdoor toilets and the ones once used in Australia was that in the village you had to walk outside to the sound of howling wolves.

I can only imagine how much of a culture shock it must have been for both of my parents when they moved to Perth.

*

In March 1978, a beautiful love story began. That's when my mother and father first crossed paths, thanks to a mutual friend. Dad met my mum on a trip back to Macedonia when he was twenty and she was nineteen. It didn't take long for them to realise they were meant to be, as they got married three months later, in early June.

They didn't have a wedding, they just signed the papers at a registry office. A few months later, in October, they started their life together in Western Australia. They only knew each other for a few months before deciding to get married. Then Mum moved to the other side of the world from her family to start her new life with Dad. Sounds strangely familiar, doesn't it?

She left everyone and everything she'd ever known. She didn't know anyone in Perth except her new husband, and she didn't speak a word of English. Let's not forget this was before FaceTime and Facebook, when international phone calls cost a small fortune and letters took months to arrive. It was such a brave thing for my mum to do. She never struck me as a risk-taker, so the move was huge for her. Mum took a massive chance, and I'm glad she did.

*

As immigrants, my mum and dad shielded me and my older sister, Lidija, from a lot. They did the same with our younger brother, Robert, who was born seven years after me. They never wanted us to worry about anything – they taught us to go with the flow, and that things weren't a big deal (even if they were).

When I was four years old, well before Robert was born, my parents made the decision to return to their homeland, so they moved our family back to Macedonia. They built a white two-storey house in the charming town of Ohrid, not too far from the picturesque Lake Ohrid centre. While the house looked similar to others in the area, it was a humble two storeys – others were three to four storeys, which was in fact a standard-sized house for many, as the floors in most homes housed various generations – families could live together under the one roof but still have their own family space. It was almost like everyone had their own little apartment blocks and when they grew up and got married they could choose to live under the same roof but on their own level. There was something magical about our house, which was nestled against a neighbouring orchard and fields with incredible views of the nearby mountains. At night, the lights from the distant villages twinkled and lit-up crucifixes stood tall and strong in the darkness.

There was a small, marbled entryway leading to the kitchen and living area where so many wonderful memories were made. The kitchen had a magnificent rustic woodfired oven and stovetop which were the heart and soul of the household and provided warmth in the colder months. Next to this was the living room which hosted joyous family gatherings, with many laughter-filled conversations and the sound of clinking glasses.

From the second-floor windows we could see the beautifully illuminated fortress of Tsar Samuel perched in the distance. As a child, I would marvel at its splendour. As I matured, the lights would still captivate me, but now they transformed into more than just a visual spectacle. They became a catalyst for igniting an inner dialogue about life and how magical it could be. That, and dreaming up the perfect outfit for an upcoming beach trip and thrilling night on the town – a blend of teenage daydreaming and an appreciation for the profound beauty that surrounded me. When I was there our family home became a gateway to dreams that I thought would never see the light of day, but ooh, what magical dreams they were.

The village was accessible by one road that was the centre of our vibrant community. Relatives, neighbours and villagers on bikes, tractors, would ride past waving hello as they made their way to work in the city or in the fields, and cars and buses effortlessly navigated the potholes that scattered the roads which were lines with raspberry and blackberry bushes. There was no need for invitations or phone calls to see if you were home for a visit; people would simply stop by, spreading kindness and warmth with every visit. Even those in a rush would take a moment to stop and say hello. We would visit my mum's parents in their village, and it was like stepping back in time. At night, we'd have to carry a candle outside to go to the bathroom. It would be pitch black and we could hear wolves howling in the distance. Let me tell you, these were the most terrifying toilet trips I've *ever* experienced! I would be panicking about being attacked by wolves and bears while making my way to the outbox, especially knowing that their family pet and shepherd dog had been killed by wolves. It was petrifying, but also very beautiful.

Macedonia is a predominantly Christian country, so in the darkness of night, we could see crosses lit up outside churches and monasteries. In Mum's village, there were brooks from the mountains that trickled down to the crops below, and the sound of running water still takes me back there. As kids, we would walk up into the mountains with our cousins, aunties and uncles, and set up for a picnic along a brook or natural spring. We'd keep our drinks and watermelon icy cold by placing them in the streams and brooks, leaving them there to bob around and chill. It'd be so icy cold you couldn't put your hand in without it turning blue.

For lunch, Dad and my uncles would cook lamb on a rotating spit they'd make out of large tree branches gathered from the surrounding woods. They'd find one long narrow branch to fasten the lamb onto and two Y-shaped branches that would be firmly dug into the ground on either side of the fire, then the long branch with the lamb would rest on the Y branches over the fire and ash below. It would be turned for hours by everyone taking turns with a makeshift handle. Our mums would bring the bread made earlier that morning, as well as homemade cheeses and salads from the vegetables they grew. We'd lay down the picnic blankets and spend the entire day playing and having little adventures in the nearby woods and streams. I have a vivid memory of my mum and aunties doing cartwheels in the fields as us kids played. It was all so much fun.

Family is everything in Macedonian culture, and taking pride in your presentation is important, too. My mum loves to get dressed up. She loves wearing heels and always wears them when stepping out – and a wedge or a platform heel for more casual occasions. And she would always put on a little bit of lipstick to go to the corner store for a loaf of bread and a carton of milk. She taught us kids the importance of looking presentable and being respectful. When there was a party or event, Mum would have us all in new outfits. They weren't expensive, but they were new. We always looked our best.

I remember going to weddings – which can last from 7 am till well past midnight in European communities – and Mum would never take her heels off, not even for a moment, and would be dancing all night. She knew how to dress for an occasion, and she passed her love of fashion on to us kids.

After a year in Ohrid, my parents realised that raising us there might not be the best option for our future. It was an incredible place which we all loved, but the country's political and economic instability was a worry. They believed there would be more opportunities for their children in Australia. Two years after moving to Macedonia, we returned to Perth. It must have been a difficult decision.

My mum's entire family were in Macedonia, and the majority of my dad's, too. They had to leave them behind once again. My paternal grandparents were still living in Perth, and my dad bought a house in which we all lived together.

In the time we were away in Macedonia, I forgot how to speak English and had to learn all over again. The communication barrier made me become quite withdrawn, scared and self-conscious. At primary school, I had to try hard to understand what my teachers and peers were saying, and even harder to get them to understand me. I remember not being able to communicate that I needed to go to the toilet. I would stand up and try to explain, but the teacher would tell me to sit back down. Then I'd feel the pee running down my legs. It got to the point that I had a spare change of clothes at school, because I'd have to get changed regularly. Thankfully it didn't take me too long to pick up the language again.

Still, I became a very shy, insular child. Even as I grew older the fear of being misunderstood, embarrassed and teased was overwhelming. I wasn't adventurous at school despite my love for an action-packed adventure after school. In class, I never put my hand up to answer questions because I was afraid of getting it wrong and being laughed at. When the teacher would ask the class if they understood what to do, I'd look around at everyone nodding 'yes' and follow suit, afraid to acknowledge I had no idea. I dreaded sports carnivals. I was never good at anything – when we had team sports I'd always be the last one to be chosen. At lunchtime, I didn't like opening my lunchbox because I would be teased by some kids for having a 'smelly' and weird-looking lunch. Mum didn't pack us ham and cheese sandwiches; instead I opted for *ajvar* (a Macedonian capsicum spread) sandwiches or salami. I loved the lunches, but hated being teased.

*

One of my fondest childhood memories was at the beginning of autumn each year, when our family would gather to harvest the red bullhorn capsicums growing in our backyard. Everyone played a part, from harvesting and washing, to roasting the peppers over an open flame, giving them a light smoky flavour and making them easier to peel. The kids would also wash the jam jars and any other jars we'd saved throughout the year. After roasting the peppers, we peeled off the charred skin and removed the stems and seeds. We minced the flesh and used it to make *ajvar* – slowly cooking it with oil, garlic and vinegar in a large pot. The mums and dads took turns stirring for hours, cooking it down until it reached the desired consistency. Once this was done, the kids would help fill the jars. This tradition continued into my adult life and when my daughter Eve was old enough, she was able to be involved in the process. I found this was truly heartwarming.

Our religion is Macedonian Orthodox, and our churches still follow the calendar in use at the time of Christ, known as the 'old calendar'. This basically means that we follow the Julian calendar, introduced by Julius Caesar in 46 BC, which is currently thirteen days behind the Gregorian calendar. Christmas according to the Gregorian calendar is celebrated on 25 December which means that in the Julian calendar Christmas is celebrated on 7 January. What did this mean for me and my family? We celebrated both! Having emigrated to Australia at a relatively young age, my parents adopted the traditions on the country they called home, Australia. For as long as I can remember we have celebrated Christmas on 25 December ... and then again thirteen days later.

So we wouldn't grow up as spoilt brats, all the gift-giving was done on 25 December, followed by a Christmas lunch consisting of a lamb on the spit in the backyard with my dad's secret marinade recipe. On 7 January we would go to church and have another family lunch to celebrate. However, somewhere along the way as my parents became grandparents, the gift-giving somehow has extended to both. Nothing extravagant. Somehow, my parents' grandchildren receive gifts for both and we never did?! Now if this isn't a win for any child, I don't know what is. I feel really ripped off here!

We also celebrated Easter twice. We celebrated Easter just like most people in Australia with Easter breakfast and lunch and Easter egg hunts in the garden. Then we also celebrated the Orthodox Easter. We attended Saint Nikola Orthodox Church on Holy Saturday late that night, around 9–10 pm. When I was a kid this was the place to be – midnight mass on the Eve of Easter. We always made sure we had our best new church outfits ready! This wasn't just Easter mass, it was the social event of the year for most orthodox teens and young adults. We'd enter the church with our family, light a candle and kiss the saint icons while making the sign of the cross with our right hands, bringing our thumb, index and middle fingers to a point to symbolise the Trinity, while the ring and little fingers are pressed down into the palm to symbolise the dual nature of Christ. The motion goes from your forehead to the stomach or chest, then from the right shoulder to the left shoulder, symbolising the cross of Christ. Then we ditched our parents and hung out outside the church. I'm not really sure what was happening inside the church because I was always too busy socialising. (I know, shocking!) Before midnight the Church procession would continue outside with all lights turned off, and then we'd light and hold candles outside in the darkness with hundreds of others gathered to celebrate the resurrection of Jesus Christ. The procession around the church was led by the clergy. At midnight the church bells rang and the priest announced the Resurrection using the phrase '*Hristos Voskrese*' (Christ has risen) to which the congregation responds '*Vistina Voskrese*' (Indeed he has risen).

At Easter the streets surrounding an Orthodox Church are littered with red eggshells. Why? Because Orthodox egg cracking begins, a traditional game played with red-dyed boiled eggs, symbolising the blood of Christ and the promise of eternal life. We played this with everybody and anybody, each person holding an egg and trying to crack their opponent's egg without breaking their own. The person whose egg remains intact at the end is considered to have good luck for the coming year. Now, because every Orthodox mum felt the need to dye on average ten dozen eggs to give out, then also receive them from others, it meant that for the next week every Orthodox kid's meal consisted of eggs. How many variations of egg salad can one kid eat in a week? And the egg burps that followed ...

This not only brought our family together, but also our community. There's something peaceful and joyful about feeling a part of something like this. Being a first-generation Australian with Macedonian parents is a unique position. We were tagged as 'wogs', which I actually don't mind. It doesn't offend me if used as a loving nudge, in fact, it's something I am proud to be, even though it signifies I'm not quite a 'full Aussie'. Then, flipping the script, when you visit Macedonia, suddenly you're the 'Aussie', despite knowing every word to the traditional songs and craving your family's homemade *gomleze* (pie).

*

While I cherished my home life, at school I continued to endure a lot of teasing. It wasn't from all the kids, though. It was a select group of relentless kids and made my school experiences negative ones. Even when I was having a good day. I remember quite vividly being teased about my legs and how dark they were, especially my knees. I had dark knees and it didn't help that I had a lot of scars on my knees. I've always been very clumsy, so each week I would have another scab on my knee from falling off my bike, or tripping over my own feet or an invisible rock while running. Once they healed they became dark scars, which made me self-conscious.

At one stage, the teasing happened on a daily basis. I was around eight or nine. Up until that point, I didn't think there was anything wrong with my skin colour or my legs, but according to the kids at school, apparently there was. Then there were my lips, which have always been full. Cue the fish lips taunts. Once, I saw a mother waltz up to the school, start yelling at a child and then hit her across the head with an umbrella for being mean to her daughter. I saw other parents come to the school to speak to the teachers about troublesome kids, or to tell those kids off directly.

Now don't get me wrong, I loved my primary school and its teachers. There was just that very small group of individuals who tended to ruin things for everyone.

It was the 80s, and it seemed you could get away with rousing at other people's children. I saw these things happen at school, but when I went home and told my parents about the bullying I was experiencing, there wasn't much drama over this.

'Did you do anything to make them say or do those things?' they would ask. 'Well, if you didn't do anything, don't worry about it. Forget about it.' There was no bolting up to the school. I had to stick up for myself. Looking back now, I'm quite horrified at how those parents used to behave. At the time, I probably wished my parents would've told the other kids to stop picking on me. But now I'm glad and grateful they didn't. It taught me to fend for myself and not be so sensitive towards meaningless words. They were unknowingly the foundation upon which my resilience was built.

My parents might not have been storming up to the school, but my sister, Lidija, was always there for me. She took me under her wing. We've always been very close – she's my best friend – and in primary school when I was being teased she let me play with her and her friends. We still speak every day and have an incredibly close relationship.

For the most part, I kept to myself as a kid. I stood on the sidelines. From there, I watched and took things in. At home, I saw my parents work their arses off. They each had two jobs, working in labour-intensive factory jobs by day and cleaning office buildings by night. Dad would start work early in the morning before the sun rose, and Mum would come home at 3 pm to cook an early dinner for us kids before heading off to work again at 5 pm until 10 pm.

Because our parents worked so much, we spent a lot of time with our paternal grandparents. Dedo (Grandad) was a jolly man who always made jokes and played with us and came to school assemblies. Baba (Grandma) was more serious but would wrap us up in cuddles. There was always somebody there for us. It was a full house, but I liked it that way.

I knew a lot of the other kids went away every school holiday, taking a flight and going somewhere exotic and new with their families. We didn't. My parents had to work and couldn't take the time off. Luckily we had our grandparents living with us and looking after us during these times.

Even though my parents worked during the week, I never felt like I was missing out on anything. Come the weekends, we would go to local beaches or pools, visit wildlife parks, reserves and limestone caves. We'd have picnics with family and friends or take short road trips to Bunbury and Manjimup to pick walnuts and chestnuts from the trees. But every two to three years, we would travel to the other side of the world and go to Europe to visit our family and stay in Ohrid. We always had the best time, every time. We would go for three months and spend our days at the beach, or in the mountains having picnics and backyard (the fields) and neighbourhood adventures. And it would be amazing.

Our parents worked hard to make those overseas trips a reality for us kids, and that hard work ethic definitely rubbed off on us. I was thirteen when I got my first 'official' job, at a hairdressing salon every Saturday.

I started with sweeping, making coffees, washing and cleaning up used colour bowls, washing, drying and folding the towels and restocking products, then I graduated to washing hair and applying colour and/or perming solutions at the basin. I made eight dollars an hour, and I really enjoyed it. I was never afraid of hard work because it's all I'd ever seen and known.

Throughout high school, my parents worked for a cleaning company and my sister and I would go along once a week cleaning a twenty-something-storey office building at night. At first it was a bit of a novelty, but eventually it became real work. We had to empty all the office bins, vacuum and wipe down desks on a select group of floors and then on fourteen of those floors, we'd have to clean the bathrooms. Six toilets a floor, and four basins plus restocking toilet paper soaps and mopping. My sister and I helped with all the jobs, scrubbing toilets and basins until they sparkled. We started going more often to help out. Sometimes I wanted to clean with my parents; other times I didn't – I was tired, couldn't be bothered, but I still went. We saw how hard our parents worked and wanted to help in any way we could. Besides, how else were we going to beat our cleaning speed record? We tried to get faster and faster and faster every night. It was a challenge to be quicker but still do a good job, and that became my motivation. It was weirdly fun and we knew it meant our parents wouldn't be home late. With all four of us on the job we shaved that time down by half. It was only ever Lidija and I who did the cleaning jobs. Robert was too young, so he stayed at home with our grandparents.

Friday nights were the best in the office building because the workers on Level Seven had a party every week with drinks and pizza. I couldn't wait for those Friday evenings. There was a pool table in the bar area and lots of mess everywhere. Sometimes it was annoying if the party went on too long and we had to wait for people to leave, but it was always exciting. I used to rattle the bins to hear the cans and bottles clink. I loved cleaning up all the junk and emptying the bins. There was something satisfying about it.

Back then, I didn't have any role models with amazing careers or high ambitions. My parents were labourers and our world was quite small. Everyone around me – aside from my teachers at school – was in the same position. I wasn't exposed to other industries or opportunities. It's hard to chase a career in something that you don't know exists. In fact, it's hard to chase a career in anything other than a blue-collar job when that's all you've been exposed to.

I don't always like change. I'm a creature of comfort. Change scares me, but it's something I've had to get used to. This life has thrown so many things at me. Curveballs and chances. They mostly haven't rolled in gently; they've been hurled at me with full force.

I spent much of my early life being scared to try new things. Fear of change or failure can be paralysing. But you can't let it hold you down. I've learned that when I'm scared to take a chance in something, it's usually the right thing to do. Amazing things can come from the unexpected.

When you break down the barrier and get to the other side, it's such a huge relief, like a weight being lifted. The obstacles we face make us who we are. It's in those moments – when we're breaking new ground to get to the other side – that we grow the most.

Over the years, I've had moments when I could have stomped my feet, screamed or given up, but that wouldn't have changed anything. When you know you can't win, kicking and screaming doesn't get you anywhere but further down. There are some things we simply cannot control, no matter how hard we try or how much we want to.

In life, I've learned to just go with things, to manoeuvre around the curveballs and embrace the chances. To suck it up, bite the bullet and roll with the punches. To enjoy the little things and make the best of the situation in front of me. These are the lessons I'm sharing within the pages of this book – the lessons that have helped me through and kept me going.

This is my story, the experiences that have made me who I am. It's about sharing the real untold moments, the ups and downs, and everything in between that has shaped my path. I'm laying it out, not because I want people to feel sorry for me, but because I believe there's something valuable in being real about life. It's my way of saying, 'Hey, this is me, this is what I've been through, and it's all contributed to the person I've become.'

It's about finding strength in the ordinary, learning from the challenges, and moving forward, always forward.

CHAPTER 2

ON FREEDOM

I hated high school. It was a very challenging time for me, which I feel would have been made easier had the school lived up to my expectations. Spoiler alert ... it was nothing like the movie *Grease*! I thought it would be a fresh, positive start where I would waltz into the school looking like Sandy from *Grease* in the final graduation carnival scene. What a shake-up to my world.

My sister had told me high school wasn't going to be anything like *Grease*, but I remained optimistic, feeling she was downplaying it all. She wasn't! After this initial disappointment, the reality set in. I had very few friends and strict Macedonian parents. I wasn't allowed to do the things that most of the other kids my age did. They would hang out together after school or go to each other's houses on weekends, but being from an immigrant family, I wasn't allowed to. My parents certainly wouldn't let me go to a friend's house if they didn't know their parents. As for a sleepover? Are you kidding me! I had European parents, that was never going to happen.

I don't blame my parents. They were now navigating life in Perth with teenagers after living in a small town in North Macedonia where they were surrounded by familiar faces and knew their neighbours and the local police officers. We lived in a suburb with a lot of European residents, but it was different. My parents didn't feel the same kind of security or sense of safety.

While I wasn't allowed to eat McDonald's or head to the movies with unknown friends in Perth, on our trips to Macedonia I could run free. We were in my parents' country, they knew the place, understood how things worked and knew and trusted the people. As a teenager, I was allowed to go out until all hours of the night with my cousins and their friends because I was among family. And besides, everybody in Ohrid knew each other. It was a close community. There were three, not six, degrees of separation between people. It was as if there was always a Macedonian lady watching out for us and taking note of what time it was, who we were with and what car we were getting into. Neighbourhood watch at its finest. Or it was just plain nosiness, but either way it made for one hell of a security system. The only downfall was that you couldn't sneak in later and say you got home early. And if you had been dropped off by your crush they'd find out the truth and all the details within minutes.

We had spontaneous, exciting beach adventures on the lake. We would catch the bus in front of our house, which took us to the centre of Ohrid, and from there we would walk to nearby Kaneo, a small quiet beach nestled close to the cafe strip where we would often spend hours just chatting, drinking coffees and people watching. Other times we would make our way to the highway, where one side of the road was littered with adventurous teens like ourselves who were after a more exciting beach adventure. We were in search of beaches with music, food and bars. I stood boldly with my sister, Lidija (I went everywhere with her – I was the annoying little sister!), friends and cousins on the roadside, extending our thumbs. We had such a sense of unrestricted exploration and independence, relying on the kindness of strangers and trusting them to get us to our destination.

There was an abundance of beaches to choose from as you drove down to the winding road alongside the lake. One beach further away was a renowned party beach, Gradishte. The first time we went there we felt a surge of excitement as we stepped onto the rickety bridge that led to the unknown. As we made our way around the bridge that wrapped itself around the rock face and sat above the water, the sounds of adult conversation mixed with the sounds of children playing faded, replaced by electrifying beats of music growing louder and louder with each step. Suddenly a cave-like space came into view, a shelter for the pulsating sounds. A DJ commanded the scene, his music captivating the crowd. Bars were tucked away along the shore and a buzz of excited conversations filled the air. Young people, relaxation personified, lounged on deckchairs and towels, soaking in the sun-drenched scene. 'Now this is living,' I thought to myself, 'this is what it's all about.' The energy, the freedom, the carefree attitudes and the excitement of the unknown were a stark contrast to my Australian life.

Back in Perth, I spent weekends with cousins or a few close friends in a more traditional setting, walking the neighbourhood streets where all of our parents were close by. There was certainly no hitchhiking, no bars with deckchairs and no dance parties.

I had a few close friends at school – we called ourselves the Claws as a joke and would make ridiculous claw shapes with our hands. It was a fun, playful little group and I enjoyed every second I spent with them, so it wasn't always bad. However, one day I was walking past the area where the boys who were a year older than me sat. It was their spot; they would congregate there at lunchtime and between classes. On this day, I had to walk past them to get to my next class. As I walked by, head down, looking at the ground, the boys whistled and yelled out at me, and the older girls sitting with them just glared at me. That was it. From that day on, those girls hated me. They bullied me and threatened to beat me up. This followed me all through high school. Every day, I dreaded going to school. 'I hate this. Why do I have to be here?' I would think to myself. I spent a lot of lunchtimes wanting to run away and go home because I was afraid of being beaten up. It was a horrible and exhausting way to live.

School was torturous, and not just because of the bullying. I wasn't very academic, and that made things hard. But I don't think that spending my classes worrying about what was going to happen during recesses, lunchtime and after school with my bullies helped my concentration or academic performance. I didn't fit into the box. I learned by practice and from visuals, not from sitting and listening. I was fascinated by science and art and how things worked, and I was always asking 'Why?'. Until the teachers got fed up with the question and replied, 'Just because, that's why.' Lesson learned. I stopped asking 'why' out loud, but never stopped thinking it. I didn't know it then, but later in life I'd find out there was a reason for my struggles.

I was guided away from doing any subjects that would gain me entry to university, having been told it wasn't for me. Teachers suggested I consider doing a TAFE course instead, or just get any job I could. I was never encouraged to do more than the bare minimum of subjects needed to graduate, even in subjects that I enjoyed, like science. Their view was that university wasn't an option, so what was the point. When I floated the idea to my parents of leaving school and doing a hairdressing apprenticeship – because I liked working at the salon on the weekend – they said no and made it clear that I had to complete Year 12. Once that was done, I could choose my own path, but graduating from Year 12 was a must. I'm not quite sure of the reason, since there wasn't any pressure on me to go to university or to pursue a career as a neurosurgeon.

It seems that this significant chapter in my life was shaped by my identity as a first-generation Australian. Having immigrated from Macedonia, my parents found themselves grappling with a foreign education system. Like many immigrant parents, they placed their trust in the school system to guide, inform and open doors to opportunities for their children – opportunities they themselves had never had. They believed the teachers would recognise our potential and show us all of the paths we could take, including university.

The reality was different. The school, perhaps guided by the mainly blue-collar community we were part of, seemed to have a predetermined path for us. They saw us only for our background, that we were destined for manual labour, not academic achievement. It felt like a directive. The message was clear: our place was set and anything beyond that was unrealistic. Any dreams we had of breaking this mould were quickly deemed out of reach.

This guidance wasn't just limited, it was limiting. Despite their hopes for us to achieve more, our parents believed that the teachers better understood our capabilities and what was required, so accepted what they said as fact. If the teachers believed university wasn't for us, then it must be true. Coming to terms with this was tough not only for us, but for my parents. It felt like the dreams they had for us might never become more than just dreams. Looking back, the only thing that might have made things easier for my parents was the fact that Lidija and I would eventually hopefully marry and have kids and we'd be so busy with them that any career prospects would have been short-lived anyway.

This wasn't just my family's belief, it was common among a lot of people in our community. We were led to believe that success was a concept not designed for us. We were to follow in the footsteps of those before us, not forge our own paths. The endless possibilities we should have been encouraged to explore were instead replaced with a ceiling we were told we couldn't break. But the story doesn't end there. It's a reminder that our beginnings do not determine our endings, and the limitations placed upon us by others are not the boundaries of our capabilities.

Even though university wasn't an option, I thought perhaps I could become a police officer and a detective. From a very young age I grew up watching cop shows with my grandparents. I loved the thrill of the investigations and then the showdowns. I was probably too young to be watching these shows, but hey, I was a child of the 80s. And while my sister watched Danielle Steel movies with Mum, I was busy watching action and fighting movies with Dad – we'd watch every *Rambo*, *Rocky*, *Predator* and kickboxer movie there was. I'd always had an innate love for action – I loved playing cops and robbers with Lidija but she'd get bored with it quickly. So I'd keep playing on my own.

I wanted to be a police officer, but back then being a police officer or detective was a male-dominated profession. In high school, I once told my parents I wanted to be a police officer, and they were horrified. I was a female, I couldn't be a cop! Was I mad? They thought that if I became a police officer, I'd end up getting shot and killed. I wanted to be a detective, a really well-dressed, stylish detective, but all they saw was me carrying a gun and potentially ending up in a body bag. It was a hard 'no' from them. So suggesting the possibility of me joining the army or navy wouldn't go down too well.

I was disappointed. The only ambitions I believed available to me and ones I was 'good enough' to pursue were now squashed. (Being a parent now myself, I completely understand why they felt the way they did. I probably would have said the same thing back then.) So what was I going to do? I loved fashion, but I never really allowed myself to consider pursuing a career in this area. I didn't feel I was good enough or creative enough and brave enough for this. I had been taught the importance of hard work, but I never knew I could work hard at something I loved. Work was work; passion didn't come into it. You worked to survive and provide for your family. My parents both came to this country with nothing but a suitcase each, no money and no jobs. Both come from humble beginnings. Yet they managed to work hard and now own multiple properties, live not a rich life but a comfortable one. I don't know if my work mentality was a product of being the child of immigrants, or a sign of the times.

When I finally finished high school, I still had no idea what I wanted to do. I was seventeen and thought I was too old to do the hairdressing apprenticeship I'd wanted to do a couple of years earlier. I knew I had to do something, but I didn't know what. I was interested in different things such as fashion, science, policing and law, but I didn't think I would actually be able to get a job doing any of those things. I had my Year 12 certificate but I didn't do any of the prerequisite subjects to get into university – as I've mentioned, it was never presented as an option. Anything I had a slight interest in doing that didn't involve carrying a gun, I needed a degree for, so I decided to enrol in a bridging course to get into a university degree. That's how I started doing legal studies at TAFE. In my mind, I thought it could be a stepping stone into the legal world, and potentially into criminology. When I was in high school I hadn't even been aware that this career path existed.

Keep in mind that we didn't have the online technology at our fingertips to help us research and navigate different career paths and options back then.

In hindsight I should have worked harder to research my options, not taken no for an answer, believed in myself more and not leave my future in the hands of others.

Criminology seemed perfect, it was similar to something I wanted to do minus the gun and danger part. Halfway through my TAFE course, we went on our regular family holiday to Europe, which seemed like heaven. As always, I loved my time there, the freedom and the fun. I was eighteen, and when I came back from the trip I decided to get a job to save up enough money to go back to Europe myself. I now wanted to work and travel. It was a pretty standard goal for a regular eighteen-year-old Aussie, but I wasn't a regular eighteen-year-old Aussie. I came from an immigrant family, I was a female, and I wasn't allowed to go travelling on my own. After high school, I was in the city when someone asked me if I had considered getting into modelling and gave me their card. As much as I loved fashion, modelling had never crossed my mind. Because I was still unsure of my career path and, I admit, was looking for excitement, I decided to give the number on the card a call and went in to meet the booking agents. After that I did a few modelling classes, which I really enjoyed.

I had a lot of fun learning to walk and practising my catwalk strut. I started doing some photoshoots and shows and became friends with one of the other models. She was always off on modelling jobs, here, there, and everywhere – and she was making a lot of money. She lived and breathed the modelling world. I didn't, but I thought it could be a way for me to make some money too. She encouraged me to investigate going overseas with her for work, and my booking agent agreed it would be good for me to go somewhere with more opportunities. I knew it would be a great experience, but I also knew there was no chance in hell that it was going to happen. I was legally an adult, but not in my family. Still, I asked my parents if I could go, knowing what the answer would be. 'Absolutely not,' they said. 'You're not going overseas alone, you don't know these people, you don't know what will happen. What if you get attacked, or hurt or killed?' It all came down to me being a female. In Macedonian culture, it's a man's world. Men have more freedom, that's a cultural norm. Men can do what they want, but women have to stay at home and play house. Even though my baby brother was seven years younger than me, he was allowed greater freedom, purely because he was a male. When he was at university, he ended up doing an exchange program and living in Germany. Every weekend when we called him, he'd be in Paris or London. He had the best time, and he had all the photos to prove it. Looking over his happy snaps, I was glad he got to experience all that he did – at least one of us did and I got to live vicariously through him. But I couldn't help wondering, 'Why weren't we allowed to do anything like this?' Having said that, by the time Rob was at university the internet was well and truly a part of our everyday life. He had the information at his fingertips and could explain it all to my parents, which gave them a better understanding of what he'd be doing. He is also a genius in his own right who now has multiple degrees in business and mechanical engineering, as well as his own companies based in Australia and Ireland.

There was no exchange program for me or my sister, no end-of-school trip or parties, either. A lot of the things I wanted to do in life – from policing to modelling – weren't a possibility for me, purely because of my gender. It felt like I couldn't win. I couldn't be in a male-dominated profession like policing or a female-dominated industry like modelling. What could I do then? I did try to challenge my parents at times. My sister, who was the eldest, was well behaved. Because I was the younger daughter, I pushed back. If my parents said we weren't allowed to go to a particular party on the weekend, my sister would accept the decision, but I would argue with them for hours. 'But why?' I would ask, in the same way I questioned my teachers at high school. 'Why can't I go to the party? Why? Why?' I'd keep this up until 11 pm, even after the party would have well and truly started to finish up.

In my parents' eyes, I must have been problematic. They probably thought I was a real pain in the arse for always arguing with them, but I was really just chasing the freedom I had been given a taste of in Macedonia. It was very frustrating as a teenager trying to wrap my head around how different life was overseas compared to Australia. In Macedonia, I could do as I pleased. But at home, that freedom was taken away from me. My sister accepted how things were, but I didn't. I would argue the point, but I didn't often win the arguments. What my parents said, went. For the most part. At eighteen, I started seeing a boy my parents didn't approve of, primarily because we were constantly breaking up and getting back together. It wasn't until I was twenty-three, when I returned to Ohrid with my family, that I was allowed to stay on in Macedonia for longer with my uncles, aunties and cousins. My parents approved only because they knew I needed a break from my turbulent relationship. In hindsight the relationship was never going to work out, but at the time I was in denial and didn't want to fail or not be 'good enough' yet again. I think being allowed to stay overseas was my parents' way of trying to get me to realise that there was more to life than an on-again, off-again boyfriend. Otherwise, they never would have let me travel on my own. I wasn't really on my own, though, because I was with my relatives. I mostly lived with my aunt (apparently she and I are the most alike in personality and temperament, both firecrackers, we are!) and her family. I loved living with them. My cousins spoke English incredibly well, and I joked that they could speak it better than me. My older cousin, George, took me under his wing, taught me about the country's history and introduced me to so much culture and world knowledge.

Either way, I didn't question my parents' motives, I just grabbed the chance to stay on in Europe. I wanted to spend as much time with each of my relatives as I could.

I also stayed with one family who lived on the other side of the lake from Ohrid. They're a fishing family, so I'd go out on the boat with them and throw nets into the water in the middle of the night. Then we'd go and collect them at about 3 am – I'd be in a pair of fishing waders, pulling nets from the water in the pitch dark. It was freezing. My hands would be numb. We'd get back to shore at 5 am, and my aunty would be waiting for us with homemade *rakija* (fruit brandy) to warm us up. When she heated it up, it turned a deep orange colour. We'd be sipping on that before the sun even rose. Needless to say, my legs were a little wobbly by 6 am, but it warmed us up, that's for sure.

When it was harvesting season, I headed to the cornfields on the tractor to help harvest corn by hand. Or I'd go out mushroom picking. Either way, it was hard work – my hands would be a mess by the end of the day. But I loved working on the land and with my hands. As I've said, I don't shy away from hard work –

it's all I know – and I was fascinated by how my relatives did things.

In between fishing and farming, I also did a lot of shooting. One of my uncles, who's sadly passed away now, taught me how to clean a handgun. Or rather, he put a handgun down in front of me and told me to clean it. My cousins showed me how to pull it apart, polish it and put it back together. It was the simplicity of Macedonia I loved the most. It's not a wealthy country, they live on very little. Back then, someone's yearly salary was the equivalent of a month's wage in Australia.

There might not have been a lot of money, but there was an abundance of joy, laughter and love. Being there takes you back to the basics, and it reminds you of what's truly important: material things don't matter. What matters is spending time with loved ones, enjoying each other's company and finding joy in the small things.

It was a beautiful life, being able to open my window and see mountains, fields of flowers and butterflies; walking down the street and stopping to say hello to every neighbour; sharing a meal made from fresh veggies from the garden. That's what it's all about. I'm sure my parents hoped that I would meet a man in Europe whom I would go on to marry (and forget about my Perth boyfriend). As it turned out, I did meet someone. He was a professional footballer. He would fly over to Macedonia and we'd meet up and spend time together, then he'd fly back home to Switzerland. I thought he was great. After a few months, the footballer rang my aunty (whom I was staying with) and my parents, and told them that he really wanted me to go to Switzerland with him to meet his family. He asked for my parents' permission, and realising he must be serious about me, they left the decision in my hands. The plan was for me to go to Switzerland, to visit him and meet his family, see how he lived and stay there for a while. Days before I was due to leave, though, I got a phone call from a Swiss phone number, so I assumed it was him. It was a woman on the line. She told me that she was the footballer's girlfriend and was pregnant with his child. They had been in a relationship for some time, and I was the other woman. I was in complete shock, furious at him, sad for her and frustrated at myself for not having known. I was completely oblivious. There had been no signs, no red flags. I don't know how the footballer thought he would get away with it – the audacity was astounding. What an arsehole.

I rang him immediately and told him about my surprise call. 'I don't want to hear any excuses. I don't want anything to do with you. We are done. Don't ever call me again,' I said. Still, he tried calling me over and over again – and even called my aunty – but it was too late. I never spoke to him again. After that happened, and some time passed, my parents started asking when I was coming home. Was there a reason I wanted to stay? I didn't have an answer to their question, besides that I was just enjoying myself there. But I knew I had to get back to reality and start working again. I decided to return to Australia. I'd been away for a year and was missing my family.

The footballer flew into Macedonia the day before I left, but I refused to meet with him. I'd come to the conclusion that all men were arseholes, and he was currently at the top of the list, but I had no idea what was waiting for me at home.

CHAPTER 3

ON THE DEVIL YOU KNOW

At the age of 24 I found myself back in a relationship with my on-again, off-again boyfriend. Then I found out I was pregnant. I didn't know it at the time, but falling pregnant was the best thing that could have happened to me. Once my daughter was born she gave me a new sense of purpose. If it hadn't been for her, I would have stayed in the hopeless situation I felt stuck in. I thought that the life I was living was as good as it would get for me. I wasn't happy, I didn't have anything to look forward to and I'd lost all ambition – my dreams seemed beyond my reach. My self-esteem and self-worth were shattered. I couldn't see a way out, or even a stepping-stone in the direction of a way out. When I had my daughter, instantly it all changed.

This pregnancy was such a scary and exciting time. I had no idea what to expect. I felt tired and nauseous all the time, and the smell of meat made me feel even worse. I was experiencing strange, cramp-like tightenings of my stomach, which I eventually learned were Braxton Hicks contractions.

My boyfriend and I decided to get married shortly after finding out I was pregnant. By the time we got married I was five months in. My family was very supportive of me during this time, knowing I was married but still alone. I spent weekends on my own wondering where he was, because he would disappear for days.

About five weeks before my due date I went to the bathroom and was confused by the fact that I heard a little trickle of what I thought was pee. But wait, I hadn't even started peeing yet, it couldn't be my waters breaking because I thought that was a more dramatic gush, isn't it?! Confused and unsure, I called the nurse I'd been seeing, and she told me to make my way to the hospital. When the doctor examined me, he insisted I stayed in hospital to rest as I'd only lost the smallest amount of water and there were no signs of any labour contractions. They felt they could delay me giving birth for a while longer, possibly weeks, if everything went according to plan.

Lying in that maternity ward bed day after day, watching the other women on the ward being doted on by their partners during numerous visits a day left me feeling unloved and alone. My then husband only visited me twice for a few minutes before leaving again. I was grateful that at least my family visited me. The other pregnant women in my room would also venture out and chit-chat but I was too depressed to leave my bed. The nurses would come to check on me, worried that I was so isolated and feeling down. I started insisting that I wanted to go home, and eventually they agreed.

So I checked myself out of the hospital and continued resting at home. By 'resting' I mean I was 'cleaning and nesting', preparing for my baby. That became my focus – a great distraction from a life I felt alone and miserable in. My waters broke for the second time four weeks before my due date, and this time the Braxton Hicks contractions started to become more frequent and painful – which could only mean one thing, I was in labour.

My then husband refused to drive me to the hospital, so I held my breath, braced myself, grabbed the keys and hobbled into the driver's seat. There I was, driving myself to hospital while in labour, not exactly the way I thought my journey to having my first child would play out. When I got to the hospital, they took me upstairs to the birthing suite straightaway.

I sat upright on the bed while the nurses placed the monitors over my belly, and the doctors came in to examine me. They told me to sit back and try to relax as I wasn't fully dilated and it would probably be a couple more hours. Even so, my contractions were now becoming very painful, like nothing I'd ever experienced before. I was in pain and terrified about what the next few hours might bring. The pain in my lower back was getting worse with each contraction and this was only the beginning – how much more painful could it possibly get?! My then husband came and went; I'm not even sure what he was doing, all I know is that he wasn't there with me.

I was in the room alone, whimpering and trying to reach for something to hold onto for support with every new wave of pain. A nurse periodically popped in to check on me and wondered aloud why I didn't have anyone in the room with me during my labour. She offered me some pain relief, but it didn't agree with me, and I started vomiting violently. All they could now offer me was gas. By the time my then husband came back I was fully dilated and ready to push. I had the nurses and doctors ready to help welcome my little baby into the world.

In the middle of an oncoming contraction, another doctor walked in and politely asked if the student doctors could come in and observe. By this point I didn't really care any more, plus I didn't want to seem rude so I nodded my head and let out a quiet, pained, 'Yeah, sure.' A large group of students walked in and stood around the end of the bed looking at me wincing with pain. I went from having no one in the room to having a room full of students.

*

When I first laid eyes on my baby girl, Eve, I fell in love instantly. I couldn't help but think she was the world's cutest little monkey. That glimpse of her smooshed, adorable newborn face was all it took for 'Monkey' to stick as her nickname. Truly, she was the spitting image of the cutest baby chimpanzee, minus the fur and the tree-climbing skills, of course. That's the tale of how Eve became my beloved Monkey, stealing my heart with her irresistible, squishy face and sparking a lifetime of giggles.

Cradling her in my arms for the very first time was indescribable. She was real and unbelievably mine. She seemed so fragile I was worried I'd hold her too tightly and hurt her. So many questions danced through my mind – 'How should I cradle her? Am I doing this right? Is this really happening?' – but at the same time, with her little eyes looking up at me trying to adjust and take in her new world, I fell so deeply in love in a way I had never experienced before. I was in awe of my precious little baby girl, and this feeling grounded me in the magic of the moment we were sharing.

While we were still in the birthing suite, the midwives placed Eve in a little bed beside me. The nurses seemed to have disappeared and hadn't returned for a while. I didn't know what to do. Maybe I was meant to head to my room as soon as I was ready (nope, I was meant to have been wheeled down in a wheelchair, but I'd just had my beautiful baby girl, I was preoccupied with staring at her, so I missed this memo). There I was, getting myself dressed and pushing Eve's little bed along the corridor, searching for our room. 'What are you doing!?' a nurse exclaimed, a mix of surprise and concern in her voice. 'You're not supposed to be up and about; you just gave birth less than two hours ago you, should be resting.' I was clueless about that – I thought I was simply doing what mothers do, getting on with the nurturing and care my heart was so eagerly set on.

Of course, being from the European community, every person I've ever crossed paths with came to visit Eve and me in hospital. The last thing I felt like after going through labour and birth was seeing people. I didn't know what the hell I was doing. I woke up in the morning after having Eve, did my hair and thought, 'Okay, bring on the wogs.' They came, one after the other. Everyone wanted to see my precious new baby, congratulate me – and give me lots of advice and opinions. I had a barrage of information coming at me which I appreciated, but it was confusing as a first-time mum. They all had different opinions on swaddling, wrapping, side-lying, back-lying, etc, etc. I just wanted to do what the nurses and my mum were telling me to do. I thanked everyone and told them I appreciated all the information.

I took things onboard, but ultimately, I just went with what I felt was right for Eve. I fumbled through those early days, and tried to listen to myself and trust that I was doing okay.

*

From the age of eighteen to twenty-five, I had been going back and forth with Eve's biological dad. I tried to leave the relationship – and knew that I had to – but I kept getting pulled back in. It was Eve who stopped the cycle. Having her made me realise that I deserved better. SHE deserved better.

This time things were different. I wasn't thinking of me, I was thinking of Eve. What kind of life did I want for my baby girl? I wanted her to grow up with dreams and ambition, without all the pressure and limits I had. I didn't want her to grow up in an environment that was not suitable for a child. I wanted her to look up to me and know that whatever life throws at you, there's always something you can do to make things better. Your life is yours to live the way you want to live it. More than anything, though, I wanted her to be happy.

At that point in my life, I felt like I had hit roadblock after roadblock. I wasn't happy. Whenever I wanted to go somewhere or do something, there would be a 'no' in the way. Whenever I had an idea or a dream, there was a teacher unknowingly clipping my wings or a parent wrapped in concern, cautioning me against the wind because I was a girl and my safety was their primary concern. The few friends I had weren't ambitious. Most of all my self-esteem had taken the greatest hit and I realised the only barrier really holding me back was *me*. I was my own worst enemy. Years of being told I wasn't good enough and being repeatedly put down and cheated on broke me down. I believed it. I was a shadow of myself. I didn't want any of that for my daughter. As I looked into her innocent eyes, I vowed to rebuild myself. I wanted to raise Eve with the knowledge and the belief that she could *do* whatever and *be* whoever she wanted. She was in control of her own destiny and to do this I needed to take control of mine.

*

Before I fell pregnant with Eve, there were many times when I wanted to move out of home and live on my own. Obviously, I wasn't allowed. 'You will live under this roof and you will not leave until you are married,' my parents insisted. I'm not going to push the same rules on my daughter. I want her to be able to go out on her own, so she can learn to be independent and never feel that she has no options. But more than that, I wanted her to be confident, and I didn't want her to be exposed to a relationship that wasn't working, which may have given her the impression that that was what love and marriage were. They weren't!

I wanted so much for Eve, and I knew none of it was going to happen if I stayed in this marriage. That's the reason I got out. Eve gave me the strength to leave. I needed to do more with my life, for myself and for Eve.

It was one of the hardest things I've done. I understand why so many people stay in situations like mine because they're too afraid of the unknown. Where will I go, how will I provide for my child? What if I'm just being dramatic? What if things get worse if I leave? What if this *is* the better situation to be in? It's a terrifying position to be in but I knew what was happening in my marriage wasn't right.

Back then in Macedonian culture, it was embarrassing, shameful and disgraceful for a woman to leave her husband. It wasn't the done thing. Because of the situation I was in, though, my parents supported me. They told me they would rather me leave him than for me to stay in this kind of relationship. I'd become a dental nurse and hadn't worked since a few months before I gave birth to Eve. How was I going to support us and look after her alone? 'Where will I go?' I said to my parents.

'You can always come back home, our door is always open,' they said. I had been wanting to leave my relationship for a while, but it wasn't until my parents invited me to live with them that I worked up the courage to do so. If I hadn't realised how bad a situation I was in and the negative effect it would have had on Eve growing up – I don't think I would have left when I did. I might have stuck it out for years and years. Eve gave me the courage and my parents gave me the support I needed to leave. It was a step in the right direction.

I never wanted to disappoint my family. I had been pretending everything was okay in my relationship with my then husband, despite their concerns. I'd married him because I didn't want to embarrass my family by having a child out of wedlock. It meant the world to me knowing my parents were happy for me to come home. 'I can do this,' I told myself repeatedly. And that's exactly what I did.

Before Eve turned one, we left with the clothes on our backs and moved to my parents' house. I didn't have a job, I didn't have any money. I had to start again from scratch. With a little baby. It was tough, but at the same time I was grateful to be living with my parents. It was the best thing I could have done for Eve. I was glad she was growing up with a strong sense of family, surrounded by people who loved and cared for her. It wasn't just me and Eve, there were my grandparents, my parents and siblings and their partners – and they all adored Eve. It was amazing for her to have that.

Still, I hadn't imagined raising a child in my own childhood bedroom. Even though I was an adult and had a baby of my own, I was still my parents' daughter and they treated me as such. They never said, 'I told you so.' Sometimes your parents do know best. Getting married was a way for me to get some freedom, but it hadn't worked out like that.

In many ways it felt like being back at square one. But I was back with a newfound knowledge. Becoming a single mother – and pushing past the fear and jumping into the unknown – was an eye-opener for me. I realised life was better on the other side. I didn't have to make up lies to save face, and I wasn't on my own. It was only after leaving the relationship that I realised it was never going to work out.

Once I made the decision to leave, I knew there was no going back. It wasn't going to be like all the times before; I wasn't going to return to the relationship in a few months. This time it was definitive. I was done. I walked away and never looked back.

CHAPTER 4

ON RISING FROM THE ASHES

I'm still immersed in Macedonian traditions, while outside I engage with the Australian lifestyle, forever navigating between these two distinct identities. It's an identity ping-pong match. Where do I fit? The question bounces back and forth and it's the family gatherings, the dances, the Easter egg battles and the warmth of midnight mass that bring a sense of belonging. These moments, filled with laughter, sometimes awkward dances, and always speaking in our own hybrid version of English and Macedonian. All of these experiences enrich my life, offering a unique perspective and a strong sense of self. Embracing this varied identity is not just about finding a place where I fit in but about valuing the journey.

Moving back in with my parents turned out to be a blessing in disguise for many reasons, especially for Eve.

It opened up cultural experiences she might have missed out on otherwise. Imagine the magic of celebrating not just one, but two Christmases and Easters, each with its own unique flavours and traditions. She could see the beauty of our heritage up close, from honouring Saint name days and going to church, to the whole family generational event that is making *ajvar*. It's like having a front-row seat to the most vibrant, colourful show – one that roots us deeply in who we are and connects us across generations. This involvement in our culture isn't just about preserving traditions; it's about passing on a legacy of identity and belonging.

As a proud Australian Macedonian, family is everything to me. In this kind of household, the concept of quiet time or having your own time and space rarely exists. Like it or not, we're constantly in each other's space, in each other's business and we're always talking over each other, speaking in significantly higher decibels than the average person. To an outsider, it seems like we are always yelling and arguing. We're not! That's just how we talk.

Every conversation is 100 per cent passionate and animated. I loved it even when I hated it. I know it took some time for Sam to adjust to this, asking, 'What's wrong? What's happened? What's going on? I'd look at him, confused, and say, 'Nothing, we're just talking, why?' He'd look at me, bewildered and even more confused than I was.

In my family home there was always an abundance of home-cooked meals, a buffet of choices that were amazing, but be warned – if you were to ask for a small serving of anything you would feel the wrath of my mother. That's how I grew up, and it was how Eve was going to grow up, too. Being back under my parents' roof as an adult with a baby was an adjustment, but I welcomed it wholeheartedly.

In some ways being a newly single mum felt liberating. In that moment I let go of so much unnecessary stress and worry. I knew it was going to be a shitshow ahead, but at least I had my daughter and my family around me for support, and it felt like I was taking back control of my life and my future.

Both my parents worked (and still do) long hours and physical jobs. During those first few years, I spent every minute I could with Eve just chatting and playing. I loved watching her discover new and exciting things.

She'd make me laugh all the time. One day she found some chewing gum and walked across the backyard to my parents' thriving veggie patch (... because why would you have a swimming pool when you can have a veggie patch, a touchy subject when I was a teen during Perth's long, hot summers). She sat near the edge, made a little hole in the dirt and popped the gum inside, covered it back up and patted it gently. When I asked her what she was doing, she looked at me and said in an 'isn't it obvious?' way: 'Planting a gum tree.' I couldn't help but laugh and almost cry at her truly innocent and ridiculously cute remark.

During this time my sister was already on her own journey. She had married Jason and set up a home with him. Jason embraced Eve as one of his own, even before he became a father to two daughters himself. He consistently went above and beyond to make Eve feel loved, and valued, showering her with gifts, taking her on adventures and ensuring she never felt she was missing out. During this time, Jason was always on the lookout for new and exciting activities that could bring joy to Eve, and us as a whole. His inclusivity extended even after his own daughters were born, still treating

Eve with the same affection and generosity. He made it a point to ensure equality among the three girls, never favouring his own daughters over Eve. In essence, he was a father to three girls, and I'm eternally thankful for his presence as a positive male figure in Eve's early, formative years.

So, my baby brother, whom I probably shouldn't call by that label considering his whopping, six-foot-tall frame, was also still living at home – though it felt more like we were living in his world. This guy was a legend for hitting the books as hard as he hit the dancefloor, making our house the go-to spot for his study-slash-party crew. Living with him was like riding a rollercoaster blindfolded – thrilling, but a test of patience. His approach to cleanliness was artistically chaotic. He'd make breakfast, and the kitchen would turn into a live exhibit titled 'Doors Wide Open'. It was as if he believed whatever was in the cupboards would suffocate if left closed for too long. Despite the mess and the daily dose of sibling squabbles, watching him grow up was pretty cool. He was also a super bro/uncle to Eve, dishing out a mix of playful teases and jokes, which only a brother would do, all while showering her with love and warmth. Being with him at this time, with all its mess and laughter, was something special.

When Eve was around four or five years old, I started taking her to daycare, which was conveniently located next door to my parents' house. I had part-time jobs in retail so I could finally start saving up some money for Eve's and my future. Though I was busy with my workload, I just loved being with Eve, and being her mum. She was without a doubt the joy of my life. I took her everywhere with me. We were at the park every day and played nonstop. I took her to art exhibitions and shows, anything that interested her.

I wanted more for Eve, and I also wanted to do something for me. I decided to go to university, to study and to make something of myself. I wanted to prove to myself that I could, and to prove to anyone who ever doubted me, namely my teachers and peers, that I could. I wanted to prove this to anyone who had said to me, 'Oooh, you're too old to do that now.' But the person I mostly wanted to do it for was my daughter, so she could look up to me and know that there's always something better and brighter, you just have to want it.

When one door closes, another opens. And that's how I started my university degree at the age of thirty.

It doesn't matter how old you are or what sort of situation you are in, you can always do something to improve your life. I enrolled in a Bachelor of Science in Molecular Genetics and Biotechnology. It was a maths- and chemistry-heavy course, which was interesting because I hated maths and never really did a day of chemistry in high school. I was not only learning the processes of complex chemical equations and formulas, I also had to learn the basics so fast that it made my head spin. It was crazy but wildly exhilarating.

I was one of only a few 'mature-aged' students in the degree. I remember being in lectures, tutorials and labs and feeling ancient surrounded by young kids straight out of high school. I hadn't been in school for over a decade. These kids would leave class to go home and study or hit the pub for a drink, and I'd go home to be a mum.

By this time, Eve was at school herself. In fact she was now attending the same primary school as I had, and I loved this. The grounds and some of my favourite teachers were still there. All the things I loved about the school remained.

On a few occasions when I had classes and Eve had pupil-free days or was on school holidays I would panic. The majority of my family members were at work and I'd felt guilty leaving Eve for long periods with her great-grandparents, who were slowing down, and Eve's energy may have been a little much for them for such long periods.

I didn't have any other options, though, so I figured I'd just have to take her to university with me. Excited by our latest mother–daughter adventure, she was more than happy to accompany me to university. As we walked through the large, spread-out campus, she marvelled at the sheer size of mummy's school.

Not knowing what kind of response I'd be met with, I awkwardly approached my lecturer to let him know that I had no one to leave Eve with. He was incredibly understanding and welcoming. Jokingly, he even told the entire lecture theatre that he had a new student attending, asking Eve's opinion on things throughout the lecture. The other students were also very welcoming, they thought it was adorable. She was well behaved and didn't disrupt anyone during the entire two hours, sitting next to me in the huge lecture theatre with her pencils and paper, 'taking notes' and writing down equations. She drew pictures of petri dishes and colonies like those she saw on the enormous screen at the front.

It could've been a stressful situation, but the lecturer and fellow students in my class made it easier. I'm grateful for that. There weren't any other parents bringing their kids to lectures. I didn't take Eve to lectures all the time, but when I did, it felt good knowing it was okay. It was one less thing for me to worry about. Eve was given a glimpse of university life (minus the fun drinking and partying!), which was something I'd never had growing up. And it showed her I was still at school, learning, just like her.

Sure, I could have set a better example for Eve when it came to studying. I recall teachers saying, 'Now this is a comprehensive assessment; don't start two days before it's due. Don't leave it until the last minute.' Sure enough, there I was, starting it two nights before it was due! I struggled a lot with time management, but I worked well under pressure. The more things I had to do, the more I got done. Throw it at me! I always got it done on time.

The course itself was fascinating – I've always loved science – but I was juggling so many things at the time that it often felt like I was on autopilot. There were many occasions when I'd fall asleep at the kitchen table studying at 4 am, only to wake up at 5 am and keep going.

On top of studying, I was raising Eve, working and paying my way. Even though I was living with my parents, I didn't really rely on them financially. Money was tight, but I paid for everything to do with Eve and I contributed groceries and things for the house. I wouldn't even allow my parents to buy a single box of nappies when she was a baby. It was a matter of pride for me. Or maybe it was pure stubbornness. My mum would try to pay for little things. 'Let me get this,' she'd say. 'No, thank you. You put a roof over my head, I'm getting this,' I would reply. I didn't want any handouts.

I knew I couldn't stay with my parents forever even if they wanted me to, so I worked hard to earn a living and create a positive future for Eve. Sometimes all that hard work felt pointless, though. My divorce became complicated and lengthy and, in turn, costly. So much so that I had no choice but to drop the number of subjects I was doing at uni so I could work more hours to pay the never-ending legal fees. It got to the point where I was receiving an invoice for thousands of dollars every week.

It made me feel like I was going around in circles. Every cent I saved would end up going towards these bills. It was one step forward, ten steps back. I kept telling myself I just needed to get through the day, then the week, then the month. I just had to pay the bills that were due in front of me. There was no end in sight, and that made it very difficult to remain positive and motivated. It was especially cruel because I knew that money should have been going to Eve and her future, but instead, it was unnecessarily going to lawyers. I wanted it to stop, but it was out of my hands.

Sometimes it was hard to contain my emotions. With Eve out of earshot, I would cry in frustration about the situation I was in. My family were just as baffled by the Family Court systems as I was, but would try to be calm and reassure me that everything would be okay. I'm not someone who cries often, and I'm not sure if the way I grew up forced me to have a thicker skin, or it was an innate thing, but I was able to receive a lot of blows without physically breaking down.

On rare occasions I couldn't hold back the tears, though. Eve would ask me why I was crying. I hated her seeing me upset. I hated crying; anyone who knows me knows I'm not a crier. I just don't cry, let alone having my daughter see me. That is one of my biggest regrets: letting her see how stressed and upset I was. She thought it was because I was working and studying so hard, but it was more than that. Ironically, it was because I was in complete despair at the lack of control I now had, despite believing I finally had control of my life.

I was a single mum, working and studying, trying to do the right thing for my daughter. I knew finishing my degree was important because it would eventually allow me to earn more money than I ever could working where I was at the time, but it seemed the harder I tried to get ahead, the further behind I fell.

*

Looking back, I don't know how I made it through that time. I guess I didn't really have a choice. I knew if I stopped or gave up, my daughter would end up in a position she didn't deserve to be in. As always, Eve was my driving force.

I hadn't planned on being a single mum and living with my parents in my thirties, but here I was. At the same time, I was glad to be there. I'd seen what I didn't want out of life and I got myself out of that situation. What happened to me made me stronger; it made me really figure out what I wanted for myself and my daughter. It gave me the courage to do the hardest thing in the face of stigma and shame. As I've mentioned, in Macedonian culture getting divorced is seen as a failure. I had failed. Even though it was the right thing to do, I still felt shame and guilt.

I had to let all of that go. Otherwise it might have buried me whole – and that wasn't an option.

When I had Eve, things stopped being about me. They became about my daughter and what was best for her. My life was about my daughter. Everything I did was for her; my wants didn't come into it. My sole focus was raising Eve in the best way possible and making sure she never went without.

Unsurprisingly, I didn't get out very often. I didn't have hobbies or much of a social life. I'd see a handful of friends who were also mums on playdates with the kids and occasionally go out to dinner with single girlfriends. For the first few years, that was the only socialising I did without my daughter, and it happened maybe once every two months, if that. I wasn't a big drinker, so I rarely went to bars or pubs.

After a string of retail and dental nursing jobs, I managed to find myself a job working as a scientific sales rep. The job was a step in the right direction in an area I was studying and a step up in pay. My role involved going around to different hospitals and stand-alone research laboratories, to understand the work they were doing and ascertain how I could help them with the supplies or equipment required for their work. The best part of my job was getting to meet and work with some of the most inspiring scientists in the country, such as Dr Barry Marshall, who was awarded a Nobel Prize for his groundbreaking research with Robin Warren and their discovery of the bacterium *Helicobacter pylori* and its role in peptic ulcer disease. Meeting such amazing people who were changing the world was incredible. The job gave me a real glimpse into life in science, and I loved it.

I also had the opportunity to visit some secret labs that didn't have specific phone numbers or signage. The first time I paid a visit to these locations I would have to wait outside until someone came to meet me and escort me in. It was all very hush-hush and I found it extremely exciting. I was also lucky enough to visit the police forensic labs, which was a highlight because this was an area where my interests lay.

I saved every cent I could and put some money aside for a holiday. When Eve was eight, I took her on our first mother–daughter trip to Macedonia and Paris. People might wonder how a single mother could afford that – I've wondered it, too – but it was important to me for Eve to see the world, so I made it a priority. As I said, I didn't have a social life, I'm not a big drinker and I spent very little on clothes for myself, opting to buy items I could wear with various things I already had and buy them on sale from stores whose prices were already inexpensive. Of course, I was also lucky that I lived with my parents. They didn't charge me board – they're European and this was the way things worked in their homeland! – so I wasn't paying rent, which was a huge help. It also helped that we loved spending time with each other. It was a simple life.

Because of all that, I was able to take my daughter overseas. Call it clichéd, but I really wanted to take Eve to Paris Disneyland. I booked a cute little modest hotel for us that looked beautiful in the brochure. In the photos, our room overlooked charming courtyard garden. Yep, it didn't look anything like the photos. The 'courtyard garden' was a single chair and a pot plant in a two-by-two space in the middle of the hotel. Nevertheless we still loved our hotel. Our room was so tiny that we didn't even have the space to open our suitcase if we didn't put it on the bed. The bathroom was cramped and the door almost hit the bed as you walked in.

Navigating Paris with my young Eve turned into very humbling moment for me. I was navigationally challenged and Eve was a teeny-weeny pathfinding genius. Our mornings were filled with excitement and croissants, but finding the Eiffel Tower? That became our challenge.

The tower teased us as we glimpsed it behind other buildings – it seemed to be not too far away at all. My 'expert' navigation turned a simple journey into a wild goose chase. Eve, on the other hand, seemed to have a built-in GPS. After a few hours of stubbornly leading us in circles, I finally handed the reins over to her. 'All right, fine, let's go your way,' I said, half-defeated, half-amused.

Sure enough, Eve's direction got us to the Eiffel Tower in no time. Standing at its base, I couldn't help but marvel – not just at the tower, but at Eve's incredible sense of direction. If left to me we'd probably still be walking around the Parisian streets in circles today looking for the tower. The photos of Eve beaming in front of the Tower are priceless, a hilarious testament to our navigational antics and a reminder that in Paris, sometimes the best guide is a child.

On the day we were meant to visit Paris Disneyland we both woke up feeling under the weather. We had the sniffles – we felt like we'd been hit by a truck – but we weren't going to let that ruin our plans to visit the happiest place in the world, Disneyland. 'We're doing this,' we said, as we jumped on the train, yet again compliments of Eve's navigational skills and knowledge of the train system. How a child that young understood the Metro lines and I didn't is mind-boggling! On the way there, we met the most beautiful young couple who helped us navigate our way. They made sure we were headed to Disneyland, not another country in the opposite direction, and we got along so well that we exchanged email addresses and kept in touch.

It was raining when we got to Disneyland but we were armed with our ponchos so we didn't care. We saw parades, went on rides and took selfies with our Minnie Mouse ears. It was everything we'd expected and more. I loved getting lost with Eve, making new friends, trying to understand French menus and restaurants together and walking for miles through every exhibition at every museum. Eve loves museums, so the Louvre blew her mind. Getting to spend that quality time together, getting lost and laughing was the most wonderful experience in the world.

From Paris we continued to Macedonia. I wanted Eve to spend time with the family there and to do all the things I got to do as a child. Just like me, she loves Macedonia. The first time I took her there, she was two. We went on a family holiday with my mum, dad, brother, sister and brother-in-law to Dubai, Rome and Macedonia. It was such an incredible journey seeing new places and experiencing the different cultures for the first time as a group. My time in Macedonia as a child is so precious to me, and it meant a lot being able to share that with Eve. Also, the majority of our extended family still live there and had not yet met my little girl. It was such a delightful and heartwarming experience showing her my beautiful homeland.

During this time, in my early thirties, I had a vision for what the rest of my life would look like. It was only me and Eve in that vision. I was happy with things being just the two of us. My daughter was my world, and I didn't need anything or anyone else. I saw myself finishing my degree, getting stuck into my career, moving out of my parents' place and raising my daughter to be a strong, independent woman on my own. I was focused on myself, Eve and our future.

It was just the two of us in the beginning, and I thought it would be that way forever. It was us against the world.

CHAPTER 5

ON TAKING CHANCES

It was Eve who told me I had to get out more. She'd seen other parents in relationships and coupled-up, and she wanted the same for me. 'You need to go out and have fun and meet people,' she said. It was pretty humbling getting dating advice from a kid in primary school.

One night, I caught a glimpse of Mum and Eve completely enthralled with a TV show and discussing something intently. Intrigued as to what had them both so engaged, I stopped to see ... *The Bachelor*. They were watching *The Bachelor*! 'Really? This is what you're both watching?' It seemed like the most ridiculous show. 'It's a bunch of desperate women!' I said to them.

Mum and Eve attempted to explain what was currently happening on the show, and I laughed as they told me how entertaining it was. But I wasn't interested. It was cute to see them watching it together, discussing what, how and when something happened. It just wasn't my cup of tea. That didn't stop them from watching it – or telling me what was happening in every episode.

One night after enjoying a family dinner with my sister, brother and their families, we'd cleaned up and Mum and Eve were taking pole position on the couch to find out what was happening on their new favourite show. It was Eve who first said, 'Mum, you should go on *The Bachelor*!' She'd seen commercials about applying for the new season.

'You should definitely go on *The Bachelor*,' Lidija echoed. 'This will be your last chance, next year you'll be too old,' she joked.

Both insisted I consider going on the show. I laughed it off and said, 'Seriously, it's a bunch of desperate women fighting over a guy! I don't think so.'

'It's the last day to enter to be on *The Bachelor*,' Lidija said one day. 'You really should apply for it.'

'Yeah, Mum, you have to apply!' Eve and my sister were now both adamant.

'Fine, okay, I'll apply.' They had worn me down; I wanted to satisfy Eve's repeated requests, but I didn't take it seriously for a second.

I filled out the application form late that evening at the eleventh hour. I thought applying for the show was silly and I wasn't actually applying to try to get a place on the show, so I wrote some playful answers to some of the questions. I didn't give it any thought at all. A question asked me what I was passionate about, and my response ... 'Whopper with cheese!'

I submitted the form just before applications closed and told my sister I did it. I thought that would be the last I heard of it. End of story.

Days later, a producer called me to say they were holding auditions for *The Bachelor* in Perth later that week and they'd like me to attend. In complete and utter disbelief I took down the information, still unsure if I'd actually go. When I rang Lidija to tell her I'd been invited to audition for the show, we both started laughing uncontrollably. 'Are you kidding me?' she said, knowing how ridiculous some of my answers had been on the form.

'I know, I know,' I replied, laughing.

I was still debating whether or not to attend the audition when Lidija said, 'Look, just go to see what it's like and what happens, just do it.' I'll admit, all this left me interested in what the audition process for a TV show would be like and what was involved. I didn't think I'd be selected to be on the show, but this was my chance to see how things work, so I figured I could go along, have some fun and just see what people who are crazy enough to go onto a reality dating show do to get there. And that's how I ended up at an audition for *The Bachelor* at the Convention Centre in Perth.

The audition process started with the producers getting the applicants into groups. The room was full of girls in their twenties, and I felt ancient at thirty-four. Once we were split into groups, we did some group activities. One activity involved sitting in a circle, turning to the girl on your right and telling her something you like about her, then turning to the girl on your left and telling her what you don't like about her. It was lighthearted fun, really, nothing too serious at all. But then I guess we were shortlisted, because some of us then needed to sit through an interview process. A producer conducted the interviews and he had a great energy about him, making me feel like in that moment I was exactly where I needed to be.

As the interview wrapped, I stood up, thanked them for their time and walked out of that room assuming that was the end of the line for this gal, but I was thankful for the experience because it was something I might otherwise have never had the opportunity to do. As I was walking out, a member of *The Bachelor* team directed me to go and see another team-member. I was handed an envelope. 'You need to take this and leave now, don't talk to anyone about this ... Congratulations, you're in, they loved you!' she whispered to me. 'Now go.'

In complete shock I took the envelope and walked out bewildered. Smiling from ear to ear, not because I was successful in getting a place, but at how insane it all seemed. 'What the hell is going on?' I thought to myself. 'What on earth is happening?' I let out a little laugh.

Never in my wildest dreams would I have ever applied to be on a reality show, let alone now be cast as a contestant. I wasn't meant to get the call. I wasn't meant to get the audition. I wasn't meant to get the envelope. I was the oldest woman in the room, which is quite crazy considering I was only thirty-four. But the universe put me exactly where I needed to be, I just didn't know it.

As I left the building I rang my sister to let her know what had happened, and we both burst out laughing again. 'What do I do now?' I asked her. 'What do I do, we didn't plan for this.'

I had a huge decision to make. To go on the show, or not? I really didn't want to go on reality TV to meet someone, especially when I thought reality TV was such a joke. I didn't think it was going to work for me. I felt my whole situation screamed that I wasn't a good fit: I was a European–Australian single mum in her mid-thirties. Really?!

However, that wasn't even the main obstacle in making the decision. My biggest concern was leaving Eve. I'd never been away from her, not even for a day. Going on the show would require me to leave her for a period of time. I thought perhaps I would last a week or two before I was sent home and I didn't like the idea of that; it was a long time to be away from Eve.

'Evie, Mummy applied and got on *The Bachelor!*' I told her when I got home. She was so excited for me and I had to calm her down and explain that to be on it would mean going away for a couple of weeks. 'I won't be able to see you or talk to you,' I said.

'That's okay, I'll be here with Baba and Dedo, you have to go on the show!' she said. Eve was really excited. There was no doubt she wanted me to do this, even though it meant being away from each other, something new and foreign for both of us. I wasn't sure she completely understood what that meant. Was she just caught up in the moment? Every day for a week I kept asking her and explaining that I'd need to go away for a short time, but her response never changed.

Eve was utterly supportive, and so was my sister, who told me she'd visit Eve with my nieces in tow every day, and her husband would be back from work to help out, too. My baby brother, now married, thought it was hilarious and demanded, 'Don't embarrass us!' Kristina, my sister-in-law, loved the idea and supported it 100 per cent. My parents, on the other hand, weren't as excited about it. They thought it was the most ridiculous thing they'd ever heard, as I had to begin with.

Even though Mum loved watching the show, the thought of me being on it was mortifying. 'You can't go on something like that,' she said. 'Your life will be on display. Everybody will know everything.' Mum did have a valid point. When my dad found out he said jokingly, 'What? You must be nuts!'

After contemplating it for a while and thinking about my situation with Eve, I decided that this wasn't even a choice anymore; it was something I had to do. I wanted to show Eve that you need to take chances in life and sometimes do things that make you uncomfortable. We both needed to step outside our comfort zones – these are the experiences that will make you grow and build strength and resilience. Not to mention, it might be fun. Just like the application and audition process, it could be interesting to see what happens behind the scenes of a TV program. And besides, I might meet the man of my dreams. I doubted it, but it was worth a shot. Perhaps that's exactly what I needed – producers choosing my next partner because God knows I seriously sucked at choosing them.

I had to tell my boss I needed to take a couple of weeks' leave. 'I'm just going away for a little bit,' I told him, because I wasn't allowed to tell anyone where I was going.

The day that I left to head to *The Bachelor* mansion in March 2015, my mum still wasn't keen on the idea of me going on a TV dating show, but she had definitely come around a little and was now joking, saying, 'I can't believe you're doing this,' while shaking her head at me.

I playfully joked back, saying, 'Yep, I am!'

Dad just laughed. He officially thought it was bloody hilarious.

Saying goodbye to Eve was excruciatingly painful. I told her to be good, listen to her family, do her homework and that I loved her more than anything in the world. I kissed her repeatedly and hugged her so tightly that it may have slightly squished her. Then with one final kiss and hug I told her I loved her again and I'd see her very, very soon.

I made my way to the airport with zero idea of what I was getting myself into. I'd never done anything like this before, I was completely out of my comfort zone – but I do believe that's where the magic happens. After I landed in Sydney I was met by a producer and was taken to a location where we had to all gather in a hotel conference room to sign in and hand over some of our belongings – keys, phones, passports, wallets, laptops and other electronics. We were only allowed a pre-loaded iPod shuffle. It was like we were checking into prison but with nicer surroundings. Any medication also had to be checked in and would be allocated as needed.

We then spent a couple of days settling in at some random hotel/apartment – to this day I have no recollection of where it was. We weren't really sure what was going on. We weren't given an itinerary – it was all very secretive and quite exciting. We were just told be packed and ready to go at a certain time. We were taken to another large convention room which was buzzing with activity. It was set up with hair and makeup stations at one end and a large makeshift dressing room at the other. It was somewhat of a production line of girls having their hair and makeup done while others were being fitted for various outfits. I was looking around, taking it all in. The room was filled with a mix of excitement and nerves, and we spent the entire day preparing for what was going to be the night our adventure began.

We were filming the first episode where all the contestants get to meet the Bachelor and make their first impression. It was nerve-wracking and I had butterflies in my stomach the entire day. 'Oh my god, what the hell have I done? What am I doing here?' I thought to myself. It was now my turn to try on some dresses for that first meeting. Thank goodness they had dresses like this, because I hadn't brought much with me. I was oblivious to how this all worked. They found the perfect dress for me, a long, black, almost gothic-inspired dress with a full skirt. I loved it. If I was going to embarrass myself at least I'd look good doing it!

I kept trying to tell myself it wasn't that bad, but I was terrified. I figured I would just take the lead of the other girls, who all seemed so sure of themselves. It felt like they all knew what was going on, and I had no idea. I was just going with the flow. When we were all ready – hair, makeup and wardrobe – a producer pulled me aside. 'You're going first,' they said. I just about died.

'Ahhh, oh really? That's okay, someone else can go before me,' I quivered.

'No, the producers want YOU to go first, so you need to get in the limo now,' they insisted. Was this really happening!?

My heart was racing a hundred miles an hour. It was my worst nightmare come true but I couldn't let it show. A sound guy walked up to us, explaining that we needed to get me mic-ed up. I didn't even realise that was something that had to happen. Great, perfect, so this meant the sound crew would be able to hear everything – my nervous pees would be recorded, fantastic. This was getting better by the second. But I still played it cool.

I didn't know what to expect when things started rolling. I didn't know what I was meant to say or do when I stepped out of that limo. A lot of the girls had planned 'memorable' first greetings, practising them while we were getting ready. But not me! I didn't want to do any of that. I was just going to get out there and pray that I wouldn't fall flat on my face when I stepped out of the car. As I've said, I'm very clumsy. 'Please don't fall, don't fall, walk carefully,' I kept saying to myself. Whatever came out of my mouth after that would be anyone's guess.

I walked like what seemed an eternity down a path and as I neared the house I remember thinking how beautiful it all was, with flowers everywhere, covering the hedges, and hundreds of fairy lights and candles. It was like something out of a fairytale (or a reality

TV dating show). Then I saw a man standing in the distance. It was him, the Bachelor, and he was tall, dark and handsome. Thank god for that. As I drew closer I stopped overthinking and stopped panicking. All of a sudden it was just the two of us standing there face to face (... well, it kinda was, there were also the five cameras I could see, not including the ones hiding behind the bushes with all the sound crew, oh, and the producers watching it all unfold live on screens in the production room. But other than that, it was just the two of us!).

I waltzed straight up to him with confidence as he said, 'Welcome.'

'Thank you,' I responded.

'Hi, I'm Sam,' he said as we both edged forward and gave each other a kiss on the cheek, neither one of us skipping a beat.

'Snežana,' I said simultaneously.

'Nice to meet you.' 'Nice to meet you.'

'That's a pretty name.'

'Thank you.'

'Where's it from?'

'Macedonia, can you say it?'

He tried to say it ...

I didn't want to have to do this but ... 'Can you say parmigiana?'

And that right there was our first meeting, our very first interaction. As I walked away and made my way towards the house, I thought, 'That went well, okay, yep, that went well. I hope he was as impressed with me as I was with him.'

But then out of nowhere, I don't know what happened, my mind went blank. I forgot the Bachelor's name! In fact, I even forgot what he looked like. All I knew was that I liked what I saw. When the producers pulled me aside to do a vox pop (impromptu interview on the spot), they asked me some questions – questions I couldn't bloody answer!

'So, what do you think? Do you like his eyes? Do you like his salt-and-pepper hair? What about his height?'

I had no idea. I couldn't even remember the guy's name! Let alone what colour his eyes were. I felt like such an idiot. He'd told me his name, and I had explained to him how to pronounce my name, and I thought he was hot, but why did I think this? I didn't remember any of it.

When the producers reminded me of his name later, I felt even more ridiculous. It was a three-letter name. So simple. Impossible to forget. Yet there I was ... forgetting it!

I told Sam about Eve later that same night at the first cocktail party. He asked me if I wanted a family, which is when I told him about Eve. I wanted him to know straightaway because if he felt that was something he couldn't be a part of, I would have gone home, back to my daughter. I didn't want to waste my time – or his. When I told Sam, he was a complete gentleman about it.

Even though I felt our first meeting and conversations went well and I felt strangely at ease when I was around him, I wasn't 100 per cent confident going into those dreaded rose ceremonies. There was that annoying 10 per cent in my mind telling me, 'Oooh, don't be cocky, it could be you going home tonight.'

I loved being around Sam and I knew he felt the same, and even though there was *almost* always a producer around, we managed to share some sneaky moments when no one was watching. These moments were reassuring of his feelings towards me. One night at a cocktail party he hadn't spoken a single word to me the entire evening, and through a twist of fate we passed each other in a corridor. His producers were ahead of him and as he passed he saw his opportunity, and gently put his hand on my waist to pull me closer, whispering, 'Sorry I couldn't speak to you tonight,' and kept moving along. Another time when we were on a group date and I was downstairs in the bathroom, Sam happened to be passing without his producer (clearly no one realised I was in the bathroom downstairs). We locked eyes and he immediately grabbed me, pushing me up against a wall as we shared the most passionate kiss, one that wouldn't be appropriate for a 7 pm time slot. There was no doubt that we were drawn to each other like magnets.

I enjoyed our one-on-one dates even though it was a little awkward at the beginning, knowing there were so many eyes and ears on us. Funnily enough, though, I did begin to forget the crew were there and sometimes when I did notice them, the fact that we were all working long days together meant I started to build friendships with them. So I felt more relaxed during these moments and as time went on I even stopped caring about going to the toilet while still wearing my microphone. I just thought, 'Brace yourselves, lads!'

My connection with Sam was so strong that an entire date was never aired. I was told there would be no hiding Sam's feeling for me during this date. We attempted to have a magical romantic moment of horseback riding that ended up being a hilarious attempt to control and guide the horses while talking about our future together.

CHAPTER 6

ON NEW NORMALS

So there I was, plucked from my regular mum life and thrown into the heart of a reality TV show, living in a Hunters Hill mansion. It was like stepping into a princess's fairytale. The mansion sparkled under the glow of countless fairy lights and candles, and was filled with faux flowers so convincing you'd swear they were real.

You'd think, with all that enchantment, we'd be sleeping in beds fit for royalty, right? Wrong. It was more 'school camp' vibes, complete with bunk beds. But honestly? I didn't mind. Grabbing the top bunk came with a perk: a spectacular view of Sydney Harbour. It was like waking up to a postcard every morning, making the whole bunk bed situation feel like a win in my book.

The deal? No leaving, no outside communication. Bye-bye wallet, keys and phone, hello mansion in a bubble. It was like being on some bizarre vacation where they forgot to mention you can't actually go anywhere apart from the rare outing with a producer or to film. Our links to the outside world – TV, radio, magazines, newspapers – vanished faster than my sense of time. But we had movies! It was our little slice of normal in a world that had been flipped upside-down.

Living in this bubble may sound like it was a little harsh, but it was actually quite an adventure. Every day presented something new. Looking back, it was like being in a weird, wacky summer camp for adult women, complete with drama, alliances and those confession-booth moments when you pour your heart out to a camera.

All in all, being in a reality TV show was an experience I'd never trade. It taught me a lot about myself and others, not to mention that I won the prize and now have a family of six to show for it. Not a bad gig!

The producers were absolute angels when it came to my catch-ups with Eve. They understood my need for a lifeline to my mini-me. They gave me the VIP treatment with phone calls, far more than the other contestants, because I had a child. It was like having an exclusive pass to the outside world, mum edition.

Navigating those chats without spilling any of the show's secrets was difficult, especially when you've always turned to family for advice. This time I didn't have my family there with me for guidance, so I felt very alone.

Well, actually, I wasn't alone because I always had a producer sitting two feet away, listening in on my phone calls. Even so, I always cherished my calls – all I really wanted to do was speak to her. It was all about Eve. School news? Weekend plans? Birthday dreams? Eve was just happy to chat. Back at home, my family had turned into a pampering crew, spoiling her with ice-cream and treats as if she were queen for the day, but in this case for weeks. I'd always end our calls with cheerfulness, painting everything in bright colours while silently ticking off the days until I saw her again.

On those quieter days without filming, I felt like a fish out of water, flipping around trying to find something to do. After years of a schedule packed with work, studying and parenting, this sudden downtime left me feeling a bit lost. But, looking on the bright side, it was a rare chance to press pause, breathe, and look forward to all the simple joys waiting at home. You know, planning for ice-cream outings and organising Eve's tenth birthday party.

When I had my first onscreen date with Sam, the producers decided to play a game of 'time is just a concept'. They set the stage for a 5 am start, only to surprise me at around 2.30 or 3 am with a gentle nudge and a cheerful, 'Good morning, sorry, we got the times wrong, you have fifteen minutes.'

We'd only wrapped filming the night before at midnight. So I'd had two hours' sleep and now basically had fifteen minutes to leap from dreamland to date-ready. Adventure awaits!

So, what's a girl to do? I sprang into action, throwing together an outfit that said 'planned this for weeks', slapped on what I prayed was a socially acceptable amount of makeup and attempted to shake off the cobwebs of sleep all with a smile. No fuss, ready for whatever twist the day might bring.

This was in contrast to some of my fellow contestants – if they were asked to get ready at that time and that fast, you might as well have been asking them to climb Everest in those fifteen minutes. For them, the mere suggestion of such an abrupt start was a cue for high drama, as if the request was the most outrageous thing they'd ever heard. Not all the ladies reacted like this, but there were a handful whose reactions were a mix of comedy and melodrama, making it clear that rolling with the punches was an art form not everyone had mastered.

In the world of reality TV, the mansion was like a culinary kingdom, boasting walk-in fridges and a pantry that could rival your local supermarket, perpetually stocked to the brim. And the cherry on top? We could order practically anything our hearts desired. Yet, amid this bounty, some girls found the audacity to lament over the bread selection. 'I don't eat this brand,' one declared, as if the loaf in question had personally offended her. I couldn't help but marvel at the drama over dough. In my book, bread is bread, and I was more than content to make do.

Escaping the mansion's bread wars for my date with Sam felt like a breath of fresh air, well, as fresh as it can be at 3 am. Meeting him at 5 am for a surprise sunrise hot air balloon ride was nothing short of magical. There we were, floating among the clouds, stealing moments of conversation between the orchestrated chaos of filming. Despite the producers' best efforts to capture every moment, genuine one-on-one time was scarce. We would be whisked away for 'necessary' adjustments, or pause to allow for scene changes or for planes to pass by so sound wasn't affected. All of this meant that our connection was constantly interrupted by an audience of cameras and crew. It's a peculiar challenge, trying to bond and connect with someone when you're never truly alone. Yet, amid the surreal setting and the intermittent company, those small moments when we'd connect were something I held dear.

Jumping into this reality dating show felt like being part of a science experiment where Sam was the main ingredient everyone wanted to mix with. Suddenly, I was one of twenty trying to create a spark with him. This made me wonder, 'Are my feelings real, or just a reaction to being in this bizarre situation?'

Whenever I was with Sam, there was no denying something clicked. But away from him, surrounded by the show's fake scenery, doubts crept in. 'Are my feelings just another prop here?' I found myself asking, half-expecting to find a label on them saying 'Made for TV'.

My habit of questioning everything didn't take a break during the show. Instead, it made me look closer at every laugh and every conversation with Sam. It turned out this journey wasn't only about chasing a romance; it was about trusting myself and trying to figure out if my emotions were truly mine or just part of the show's experiment. It was a wild ride, attempting to find real feelings in a place where everything else was pretty much staged.

*

Diving into trusting Sam was like suddenly finding myself wearing a parachute and deciding to jump out of a plane – totally out of character for me, especially given my track record with men, which, let's be honest, could easily be mistaken for a soap opera plot. Nearly every guy I've ever dated – from the globetrotting Swiss footballer to Mr 'I'm going on a holiday with the boys and – surprise – I'm engaged now' – seemed to have taken a secret oath to 'explore other options'. Just before that guy's trip, he was all sweet nothings and 'I'll miss you's. Then, bam, two days into his vacay, he hits me with a plot twist worthy of a daytime Emmy. 'I'm sorry, could you run that by me again?' I asked, expecting him to say he was joking. But the punchline never came. No, this was just another episode in the sitcom of my romantic endeavours. So, understandably, handing out trust for me was like trying to diet at a chocolate festival – not exactly my forte.

My motto going onto *The Bachelor* had been pretty straightforward: 'Like me or don't – either way, I'm cool.' I wasn't about to lose any sleep over someone who was practically a stranger, no matter how dreamy they might have been under the fairylights.

The producers, bless their hearts, tried their hardest to get more emotionally charged responses from me. During vox-pop moments they'd throw me some curveballs, hoping to unravel me on camera. 'So, why do you think Sam didn't talk to you tonight? What do you think that means? Do you think you might be going home tonight? What do you think about the date he had with such-and-such? Do you think their connection is stronger than yours?' But hey, drama sells, and viewers love it.

When the producers came looking, it wasn't drama they were after but a deeper dive into my emotional pool. But I wasn't expressing my emotions with all the fluffy theatrics. My philosophy? 'Accept me as I am or not at all.' Either way I knew I'd be okay.

Nowadays, it's almost expected that reality show contestants are angling for their next big break, whether that's as an influencer, brand ambassador or exposure for their business. But for a mum studying to be a scientist like me? Being on *The Bachelor* was less about boosting my profile and more about stepping out of my comfort zone. The notion that my appearance on the show would somehow enhance my credentials in the scientific community would be laughable. In fact, I half-expected my colleagues to convene a tribunal to question my scientific integrity. 'Since when does serious science involve rose ceremonies?' they'd muse. But who says a scientist can't have a little fun with the laws of attraction?

By the time Easter hopped around, I was still in the game. It was a peculiar mix of emotions, knowing Sam and I had a connection, yet watching him head off on dates with others who'd return with stories of their amazing and incredible romantic moments. It made me wonder, 'Was our chemistry as strong as I thought, or am I just the queen of wishful thinking?' This was reality TV, after all, where every date feels like a mini audition for the role of 'The One'.

Easter was a reality check. Being unable to spend it with Eve hit me harder than any plot twist the show could throw at me. Eve and I always marked milestones together, and here I was, trading Easter eggs for confessionals. It was then that the atmosphere shifted. Initially overlooked as the 'older' contestant and 'the single mum' I was suddenly on the radar. A month in, and the vibe turned frosty; the mansion felt less like a fairytale and more like a high school hallway, complete with side-eyes and hushed whispers. I navigated through the newfound animosity proving that even in the most surreal situations, I could roll with the punches and come out smiling. After all, what's a stint on reality TV if not a masterclass in resilience?

Two months in, and surprise – I was still on the show! Crossing the two-week mark had me asking producers to allow me to call my boss and sheepishly asking for more time off. I didn't have a real reason as I couldn't tell anyone I was filming the show. It was top secret. Then again at one month, and so on and so on. Honestly, I hadn't seen any of this coming.

Two months into the reality dating show and I was still standing – quite the surprise for someone who'd initially packed as if it were just a weekend getaway. Suddenly, I found myself on the phone with my boss, negotiating more time off like a diplomat. 'So, funny story ... I'm going to need more time off. Yes, really. More time off. Pretty please?'

Eve turned into a vault. The secret of my reality TV stint was hers to keep, sealed tighter than a classified file. Sworn to secrecy in a world where spoilers are currency, she was a rockstar, holding down the fort of silence with the skill of a seasoned spy.

When the journey hit the final-four mark and a home visit with Sam was on the cards, introducing Sam to Eve made me realise suddenly things were getting very, very real. Sure, on paper Sam was all-in about me having a daughter, but did he truly understand he was meeting the real love of my life? That's the next level.

My days were less 'spur-of-the-moment beach getaway' and more 'calendars for school events and playdates'. So, naturally, I was curious to see if Sam was truly prepared for a life with me and Eve.

I was full of anticipation when the moment came to introduce Sam to Eve, not just because they were meeting, but because it would be the very first time I'd be seeing the one true love of my life since I had begun filming. Our reunion was going to be in Perth's Hyde Park, our happy place, where we had spent countless weekends filled with love and laughter. The producers organised for us to meet, but they intentionally left out any details about how and precisely when. With the camera rolling while Sam and I walked through the park, I shared with him stories of the countless hours Eve and I had spent there, each step was bringing me closer to her. Then, amid the calm, a joyful shout pierced the air. 'MUMMY!!' There she was, my Eve, running towards me as fast as her little legs could and with a smile that melted my heart. To this day, the thought of that moment and the sound of her little voice brings tears to my eyes, and remember ... I'm not a crier.

In that instant, as our eyes locked and she flew into my arms, the world seemed to stand still. My heart was exploding. We clung to each other, our embrace a testament to the days apart, each kiss a promise to never let go. The magnitude of it all, how much I missed her, all the moments we hadn't shared, combined into that single, perfect moment. I was home, in the arms of my little girl, where every worry faded away and only love remained.

Sam and Eve's first meeting? Straight out of a heartwarming movie scene. I gave them space, hoping with all my heart that they'd hit it off. Sam was the picture of patience and kindness, while Eve played the role of the wise-beyond-her-years interviewer, throwing questions at him. It was a mix of adorable and impressive.

Then came another test: introducing Sam to my parents. Honestly, I was bracing for an interrogation scene, but it turned out my parents were fans from the get-go. It was a pleasant shock – not because Sam isn't a catch, but because to my family he was essentially a charming mystery man from across the country.

'He's lovely, and he's so good to you,' my mum observed, making me wonder if maybe, just maybe, this could all work out. Between Eve's seal of approval and my parents' unexpected thumbs-up, it felt like we were onto something special, reality TV quirks and all.

And then there was the sibling test – my brother and sister entered the scene, armed with questions that could make a seasoned politician sweat. They decided to lay out the full spectrum of my personality like it was an obstacle course, and let's just say, it wasn't for the faint-hearted. My brand of chaos is unique, kind of like if a tornado met a flash mob in the middle of a surprise party.

Sam faced the inquisition with the bravery of a knight venturing into a dragon's lair, except this time the dragons were keen on psychoanalysing every answer. 'So, you think you're ready for my sister?' 'You know she has a daughter, so …' They grilled him, half-expecting him to run for the hills. Instead, Sam stood his ground, proving he might just have the right amount of daring (or madness) to dive into the deep end of our family dynamics.

My brother and sister's approval was the unexpected encouragement I didn't know I needed. Watching Sam navigate the barrage of questions and scenarios they threw at him was like witnessing a gladiator match where the weapons were wit and charm. And somehow, amid the chaos, he emerged not just unscathed but with a thumbs-up from the toughest critics in the room. It was clear that if he could handle this with a smile, our little adventure was about to get even more interesting.

Despite initially not approving of my decision to dive into reality TV, my parents turned out to be so welcoming when they met Sam. They're not the type of people who would dislike someone just because I met him in a way they didn't initially approve.

I wasn't sweating on their open-hearted nature, it was more about Sam's Melbourne postcode that had me biting my nails. In my family's tight-knit Macedonian circle, everyone is basically your cousin twice removed or your best friend's uncle's son. Previous beaus were all part of this intricate social web, where my parents could pretty much trace their lineage back to the Old Country or cousin's best friend's brother's aunty's next-door neighbour's son. But Sam? He was an enigma, a mystery man without ties to any aunties, uncles or neighbours from the village.

So, introducing him felt a bit like bringing an unknown species into a familiar ecosystem. For all my parents knew, he could've been moonlighting as a spy or harbouring a secret identity. The moment they wrapped him in one of their signature, all-embracing hugs, I knew we were in the clear. It was like watching a high-stakes game show where everyone wins a family dinner invitation. Relief? Understatement of the year!

The night of the home visit, producers decided to grant us a mother–daughter sleepover in a motel that was … let's just say, it had character. There we were, two peas in a pod, catching up on lost time in a setting that screamed 'budget romcom'. It was the perfect blend of a sweet, surreal and slightly sketchy, a precious pause in the whirlwind of rose ceremonies and camera vox pops.

The home visit went better than expected, but at the same time, it was also the hardest part of my time on the show. Being home and then having to leave again was difficult. It was a reminder of everything I'd left behind to take this chance.

CHAPTER 7

ON TRUSTING YOUR GUT

A month before I applied for *The Bachelor*, a friend persuaded me to see a psychic. 'This lady is amazing,' she insisted. I was sceptical, but my curiosity was stronger than my scepticism.

I was doubtful as I sat across from the twenty-something-year-old psychic. She held my hand, then put it down and started scribbling and squiggling on a page. I sat in silence as she told me a handful of predictions, but the one that stood out to me now was her prediction about a mystery man.

The psychic confidently predicted, 'Soon, within the next few months, you'll meet a tall man. He's not from here.'

I asked, 'Not from here? Does that mean he's from Europe, America or somewhere?'

'No,' she clarified, 'he's from Melbourne. That's where he lives and you'll move there for his work.'

I couldn't believe her words. She was so specific. Too specific to be accurate.

On my way home I had a little giggle to myself and dismissed the idea of developing a crush on someone from Melbourne. I hadn't even been to Victoria, let alone moving across the country. The thought didn't seem possible to me. Still, a month later, I was cast on the show, and then I met Sam.

*

The Bachelor finale was approaching, and I was one of the last two standing. I was facing off against an unexpected intruder on the show. The producers started asking me questions I wouldn't have asked myself, and it got me thinking: 'Is he one of those guys who gets distracted by the novelty of something new? Surely not! Why is she still here – I feel they don't have much of a connection but she's still here.'

I was certain of my feelings for Sam and our connection, yet a shadow of doubt still hung over me.

On the day of the finale on a large property in the Blue Mountains, the wait to see Sam seemed to take forever, all day to be exact. This alone time fuelled my anxiety. 'Why am I waiting so long? Is he with her now? Why are they taking so long? Are they sharing moments that leave me as an afterthought?' My mind raced, questioning everything from the order in which we saw him, to the location of my room. I was staying in what once were horse stables and the other contestant was in the main house. I loved my room but was that just my laidback personality? I wasn't a pretentious princess and didn't care about these things, but was there more to it? Was I missing something? When it was brought to my attention, I started questioning it.

Despite the swirling questions, deep down I felt Sam wasn't the type to lead me on. He knew I had left my daughter for the first time to be there. He wouldn't have kept me on this journey, only to end it with a casual, 'Thanks, but you're not the one.' My time with Sam convinced me he wasn't one to play games. The idea of him choosing the intruder seemed unlikely – and not only would I be heartbroken, but the Australian public led by my furious mother holding a frying pan would be up in arms. Funnily enough, this thought calmed my nerves. But most importantly, I knew in my heart that we felt the same and I was just being confused by the noise and outside influences. I had to believe in us and stop second-guessing myself. I had to trust my gut.

When I finally got to see Sam at the finale, I was very aware of my heart beating in my chest. I almost couldn't hear him over the thumping. Luckily the cameras caught his words ...

'I can't believe what an incredible woman you are,' Sam told me. 'You are so strong, you are so warm, you have the biggest heart that I've ever come across and I just love being around you.'

My heart raced.

'My heart skips a beat every time that I see you and I just feel so lucky that this crazy adventure has brought us together. Every date we have been on, my feelings have gotten stronger,' he continued.

My heart burst.

'You were the first girl that I met and you are the last girl because I've fallen madly in love with you and I want to spend the rest of my life with you, Snežana. I love you so much,' he said.

My heart stopped.

I knew it. What we had was real and it was precious.

'I've been waiting to hear you say that for so long now,' I said to Sam. 'I've felt this amazing connection between us and you are everything that I've ever dreamed of and more than I could ever have dreamed of. And you will make this amazing role model for Eve.'

I'd met my match. On *The Bachelor* of all places!

After the show wrapped, Sam and I had to keep our relationship a secret. We finished filming in May but had to stay under the radar until the show aired five months later. It was great to be back in my normal life, but it didn't feel all that normal. We were still stuck in a bit of a bubble. The show organised for us to fly to Sydney. I would be on a red-eye flight when the airlines weren't as busy, then I'd be picked up from the airport by a driver and taken to an undisclosed location where Sam would be waiting for me. We had to stick to hidden places or just stay indoors. There was no going out for a coffee or lunch, but at least we finally got to spend some real one-on-one time together.

Sam lived in Melbourne, and I was all the way over in Perth. It was our long-distance love story. There was so much to consider. How were we going to navigate this? Could he blend into my world seamlessly? And what about me fitting into his? These questions hung in the air, unanswerable until we could step into the light together, free from secrecy. For months on end, we lived our love story behind the scenes, a reality many couples from the show couldn't withstand. Yet, we emerged stronger, hand in hand. Surviving those hidden months felt like a victory, proof of our resilience as a couple. It was a clear sign: together, we could weather any storm.

Keeping the secret was tougher than expected, though. Once everyone knew I was on the show, I still couldn't breathe a word about Sam and me making it to the end. Cue the endless questions. I mastered the art of the poker face, trying my hardest not to let slip a single hint or look guilty of hiding the biggest secret of my life. Acting like it was all business as usual, especially around my closest friends, felt like I was undercover in my own life.

The fact that I could sit miles away, on the opposite end of the country, and still trust Sam spoke volumes about him. Given my past experiences, trust didn't come easily to me, especially with Sam being in the limelight. Rumours were flying about, and sure enough, I'd get DMs about Sam being spotted here and there. Though he was free to socialise, navigating the public attention and dealing with those messages was challenging. Yet, deep down, I knew Sam wouldn't risk what we shared. Those bits of gossip? They were like sneak peeks into our future under the public's scrutiny, a future where everyone knew Sam's name, and mine too.

Back in Perth, I returned to my juggle – and added some more balls in the air. I dove back into work, hit the books at university, moved back in with my parents and picked up the parenting baton. As if that wasn't enough, I now had media duties for the show and a huge secret to keep under wraps. The show, unexpectedly, piled on a whole new level of business to my life. Balancing everything became a huge task, hiding the truth from everyone was exhausting and the guilt of keeping it from my friends weighed heavily on me.

It was almost a year all up, from the moment I reluctantly applied to be on the show to the day the truth was finally revealed at the finale. I wasn't the bookies' favourite to win Sam's heart, but I did.

What a wild ride it was. I was your everyday single mum, juggling life's curveballs, and then, boom – I'm on a TV show and falling head over heels in love. It felt like I'd been plucked from my life and dropped into a fairytale romance you only see in movies. And all of this unfolded at lightning speed, leaving me pinching myself, wondering if it was all real. After years of battling through the tough times, this was the break in the clouds I'd been dreaming of.

Stepping onto that show was a leap into the unknown, way outside my comfort zone. And guess what? I was scared out of my mind, but I went for it anyway. As I've mentioned, this taught me something huge: growth and the good stuff lie on the other side of discomfort. Waiting around? Not going to cut it. You have to chase what scares you, because that fear? It's the sign you're onto something big.

The moment the news broke, Sam and I were on the same page – we had to live together. The endless flying across the country just wasn't sustainable. So, who was going to move? I didn't hesitate to volunteer for Melbourne. Despite my love for Perth, I'd always felt a bit out of place there. Sam's life and business were firmly rooted in Melbourne, which made that part of my decision a bit easier.

However, the most important part of this decision was Eve and whether she was open to moving. How would she feel about leaving everything she's ever known? True to her adventurous spirit, she was all in. 'I just want to be wherever you are.' Her words made the decision sound so simple, yet the reality was anything but, especially given her close bonds with my family. It was a tough call, no doubt about that, but we all knew it was our path forward. This was the start of a new chapter for us.

When it came to Eve, Sam was great from the beginning. He was a friend, and they would chat and hang out. First and foremost Sam wanted to form a bond with Eve, he didn't want to just come into the picture and start acting like her dad. They'd go to the park, watch the footy together, and make fun of me, especially for my lack of sports knowledge. When I was doing things like calling a football oval the pitch, they bonded over laughing and correcting me, and their relationship grew naturally.

As Eve grew older, Sam and I explained the house rules to her together, and he helped implement them.

That was an adjustment for Eve, who had become used to getting her way if I said no by asking her baba or dedo. In the past I had tried to set boundaries, but as one would expect it was a nightmare with doting grandparents. So having someone stand beside me was new. I think it took Eve a while to realise, 'Oh crap, I'm not going to get away with everything that I used to before.' It was hard for us to navigate, but we did our best. All you can do is your best. You make so many mistakes as a parent – I've made countless – but just like everything, you learn from your mistakes.

Parenting feels like you're constantly guessing the next move in a game where the rules keep changing. You find yourself replaying moments, thinking, 'Maybe I shouldn't have said that' or 'Maybe I should have done this instead.' It's like walking a tightrope blindfolded. But here's the thing: as we unfortunately know, there's no damn handbook that comes with this job. I wish there was. We're going to question our choices, sure, but at the end of the day, all we can do is our best. That best might look different from one day to the next, and that's okay. It's about showing up, love in hand, ready to tackle whatever comes your way, learning a little more with each stumble. In this beautifully messy world of parenting, doing your best isn't just good enough, it's everything.

*

Just months after our reality TV romance aired, Sam, Eve and I headed to Tasmania for a bit of a family getaway. We stayed at this gorgeous place called Saffire Freycinet, which was as gorgeous as it sounds.

One sunny day, Sam gets this bright idea: 'Let's hike up to that lookout over Wineglass Bay.'

'Sure,' I said, not realising this was going to be a workout more intense than any gym session. Halfway up, I was melting. I tried to bail, but Sam was on a mission to get to the top. We made it to the top with me looking like a lobster that's run a marathon. But the view? Absolutely worth it.

Then, Sam asked Eve to take a photo of us with that gorgeous backdrop. Little did I know, this was code for 'start filming'. Down on one knee he went, and my brain was doing cartwheels. Sam started saying how much he loved me and what I meant to him and then he said, 'Will you marry me?' My heart was pounding, and my answer was, 'YES!'.

Turns out, Eve had known about the entire thing. Sam had already said to her, 'If it's okay with you, I'm going to ask your mum to marry me.' He'd even asked for her blessing, which is just the sweetest thing. They'd plotted this whole video proposal, and there I was, completely clueless. Sam had asked her permission to marry me, and they'd planned for Eve to video the proposal.

Immediately after the big moment, Eve said with a casual shrug, 'Oh, I pressed the wrong button. Can you guys just do that again?' Her timing? Impeccable. Sam and I couldn't help but burst into laughter. So, no, we didn't get the epic proposal video, but what we got was even better – a priceless moment of joy and a hilarious new family memory.

Having Eve there, botched recording and all, just made the whole experience even more special. It wasn't just about the question and the answer; it was about us, the three of us, truly becoming a family. That moment, with all its laughter and imperfection, was everything.

There we stood, feeling like we were on top of the world, stepping into our new lives together. It was a scene filled with joy, laughter and a sprinkle of happy tears. Who would have guessed a hike, drenched in sweat, would mark the beginning of such a beautiful journey? And to think, this whole adventure kicked off with a single rose on a reality show. Life has its own sense of humour, doesn't it?

Honestly, remarrying was never in my playbook. I was cruising solo, pretty set on the single life, and had closed the chapter on finding another partner or expanding the family. Then Sam happened, and suddenly, all bets were off.

My life had a blueprint that didn't pan out. But as it turns out, life had a plot twist up its sleeve that was far better than anything I'd imagined.

Sam and I first crossed paths in March, and by December we were engaged. Despite the rollercoaster ride of the show, with its ups, downs and behind-the-scenes drama, something in me just knew. It was like my intuition was tapping me on the shoulder, whispering, 'This is it.' It sounds so clichéd to say 'When you know, you know,' but we were living proof of that very cliché. We just knew.

CHAPTER 8

ON THE HARSHNESS OF THE SPOTLIGHT

After my appearance on *The Bachelor* my life took a dramatic turn. At first the attention had felt thrilling and being recognised on the streets was a little exciting. However, the novelty quickly wore off, giving way to a level of anxiety I'd never experienced before. I was unaccustomed to the spotlight. The move to Melbourne exacerbated this change, introducing me to a world where the paparazzi seemed relentless, and the pressure to always look put together became overwhelming. I felt like I could no longer step out in my daggiest faves without the risk that a camera lens was pointing my way at a bad angle. The fact that I could be photographed at any time on the street felt so intrusive. Strangers with iPhones stepping into my personal space eventually took its toll and my sense of self started to suffer.

In Perth, I'd never had to worry about this sort of thing. The city's laid-back lifestyle meant I could do as I pleased and I could be myself. Of course in Perth I still regularly wore makeup and dressed in nice clothes. I enjoyed dressing up, making an effort to look presentable – a principle instilled in me by my mother. The difference was that in Perth it felt like a choice. I was free to decide on any given day whether to embrace my inner sloth or look more presentable without being so closely scrutinised. When I moved from Perth I lost this cherished anonymity.

Melbourne felt like a fishbowl. After appearing on the show the freedom I felt in Perth was stripped away. Every decision about my appearance became fraught with anxiety, turning what was once a pleasure into a constant source of stress. I obsessed over details I had never previously even thought about – or if I did, it wouldn't be for more than a millisecond. Details such as how would this outfit look on camera? Will it translate the same on camera as it does in reality? Do these flats look good with this outfit? Or should I just wear heels? Heels elevate most outfits, and they would elongate my legs. I also felt compelled to wear makeup and dress up for even the most mundane tasks. It wasn't just the paparazzi I had to worry about; lots of people seemed eager to capture sneaky images of Sam and me. Some tried to be surreptitious – unsuccessfully. I preferred people approaching us and asking to take a photograph, which we'd always happily agree to. The sneakiness of some people was infuriating. The shift from living a carefee life to constant visibility was really jarring.

Also, I had to think about Eve, who was still very young. Seeing me worry so much about how I looked could affect her too. I tried to hide these worries from her because I didn't want her to start thinking she had to be concerned about her appearance in the same way. Interestingly, Eve would often spot the paparazzi before I did, casually pointing out, 'Oh, look, that guy's taking photos,' without a hint of concern. The fact that she seemed indifferent was a relief; I was truly grateful that it didn't bother her the way it did me.

Sam, ever the optimist, managed better under the scrutiny, not for a love of fame but due to a disinterest in others' judgments. But even his patience wore thin as our private moments and family time with Eve were increasingly hijacked by cameras. The relentless scrutiny became a daily challenge. I began to lose myself in the eyes of the public, constantly feeling judged and exposed.

Before my television experience, I had confidence and was self-assured. Now, the constant exposure and judgement chipped away at my self-esteem. I started to doubt my appearance, my worth, the way I spoke, feeling constantly under siege. I was sad about the loss of my privacy and freedom, feeling a deep sense of vulnerability that I had not expected. The transition from a private individual to a public figure was more than just a change of address from Perth to Melbourne; it was a profound shift in my identity and sense of self.

My anxiety escalated to the point where the thought of leaving my house became daunting. I withdrew from social activities, events and even simple interactions. I became so self-conscious about the way I spoke, remembering the producers' efforts to refine my speech. At the time I didn't think anything of it, in fact I found the whole thing hilarious. Fast-forward a few months and now the thought of this further drained my confidence. During interviews, my nerves would spike; I was terrified I'd say the wrong thing or pronounce something in the quirky ways I do, adding extra syllables here and there, just ... because!

My childhood fear of not understanding or misinterpreting questions returned. I was now second-guessing myself. I avoided speaking at all for fear of misspeaking and not speaking in an eloquent tone. Sam would often step in, covering for us both with a seamless understanding when I could only manage a nervous giggle.

I felt a particularly harsh sense of not being seen as 'good enough' during preparations for a significant event in Melbourne. While some brands had generously offered outfits, I had hoped to collaborate with a specific Australian label. They turned me down because I wasn't 'prestigious' enough – I wasn't wearing brands such as Dior and Chanel in everyday life. This was a huge blow that, along with the ongoing scrutiny, further affected me, making me feel inadequate in a world that seemed increasingly alien and unforgiving. Such encounters left me feeling judged and dismissed, a reminder of the superficiality of being in the spotlight. It was a stark contrast to my previous life.

Moments like these left little chips on my shoulders. I was angry – how could people be so superficial and judgemental? Simple joys such as shopping became stressful, as the fear of being spotted took away my peace. Despite being in the public eye, I never saw myself as a celebrity. This made me pull back from social media, even though it meant missing out on connecting with those who supported me. Negative comments hit hard, forcing me to shield myself from the pain.

I kept worrying about Eve, who was witnessing this negativity. I told her to ignore the bad stuff, reminding her that we know our own truth. I felt like a fraud! Here I was, trying to explain to my young daughter that you should never allow negative comments to affect you and alter your perception of yourself and who you are, yet I was allowing the outside world to do just that.

She learned to see through the fake perfection often shown online, understanding the difference between real life and what's posted on social media. Together, we learned to focus on what's truly important, staying strong amid the online noise. It was an eye-opening lesson about not believing everything you read.

*

From early in our relationship Sam and I knew we were destined to be together forever. We planned to get married and expand our little family. After the move to Melbourne, in 2016 we discovered that we were expecting a baby. The news filled us with so much excitement and we eagerly shared it with Eve and our closest friends, who had noticed that something was not quite right with me because I hadn't been feeling well.

During our first ultrasound appointment there was so much joy as the realisation set in that our little family of three was about to become four. We were fortunate to have an amazing obstetrician by our side who not only made us feel at ease but also made us laugh.

Soon we were faced with a challenge, though, because Sam had planned a 'boys' trip' to America. We ended up having arguments about it. I didn't want him to go. I was particularly concerned about the timing and about my low hormone levels, which had been detected a few weeks prior. I was starting to feel even more tired and unwell. Sam assured me everything would be fine and went on his trip to America.

Before I headed to one of my regular scan appointments, I had a happy and chatty phone conversation with Sam while he was preparing for a big night out with the boys. He was checking in to make sure I was okay, and he was excited to hear from me before my appointment. I told him that I'd be fine and would give him a call or text him afterwards.

As I entered the doctor's rooms, I was filled with anticipation and excitement. I greeted the wonderful nurses and staff who worked alongside my obstetrician – their presence always had a calming effect on me. I lay down on the examination bed while the doctor initiated a cheerful conversation, as he usually did, while scanning my belly. As he continued to scan, though, he fell silent. He kept scanning, but his sudden silence told me that something was terribly wrong. He placed a comforting hand on mine and in a soft voice said, 'I'm sorry.' Our little baby's heart had stopped beating.

I couldn't hold back the tears. The news had caught me completely off-guard. The doctor and nurses guided me into another room to give me some privacy while I absorbed the news. I was asked if they should call Sam to come and get me, and I told them he was in America.

After a moment I pulled myself together and listened to what the next steps would be. I needed to have a procedure – our baby needed to be removed from my body and there was a spot available the following day. I walked out of the room and to my car in shock as I tried to call Sam, longing to hear his voice. He didn't pick up. Completely overwhelmed, I wrote him a text message. The shock and grief gripped me so tightly that the words I typed where harsh, blunt and painfully abrupt. 'The baby is dead!' I wrote.

I still can't fathom why I relayed such heartbreaking news so bluntly, but I was in a state of disbelief and anguish. It felt like a heartless thing to do but my heart was numb.

I called my mum and my sister, and their worried voices resonated through the phone. Trying to reassure them, I composed myself. 'Don't worry,' I said, 'I'll be okay.' They told me to go straight home. I didn't! If I returned home by myself, I knew I would have been an emotional wreck and unable to pick up Eve from school and attend her school performance later that evening. In my mind I was left with no option other than moving forward with my day. So instead I drove to my next destination, a meeting. I needed this distraction.

Sam called while I was on my way to the meeting. With confusion and disbelief in his voice, he said, 'What are you talking about?! Why would you write something like that?' I recounted the news of our loss. The devastation echoed in his words. 'I'm coming home. I'll book the next flight back.'

In that moment, we both realised how far apart we were. Sam was on the other side of the world, my family in a different part of the country and young Eve was at school.

I parked my car and laid eyes on my friend Sal. Sal and I had started off by working together – she'd been helping me navigate the chaos that was now my world after *The Bachelor*. We'd ended up becoming friends – she was the first friend I'd made since moving to Melbourne. I walked up to her. She knew I had just come from my appointment, and I shared the news with her on that East Melbourne street. Shocked by the news, she hugged me tightly – knowing that Sam was far away.

'I'll reschedule our meeting with this client,' she said.

Without any hesitation I said, 'No! We are going to this meeting.' She looked a bit shocked – she must have thought I was crazy. But I just needed the distraction. During the meeting we behaved as if nothing had literally just shattered my heart. We laughed, we engaged in conversation, discussed our collaboration and future plans. After the meeting I had to move forward with the rest of the day's plans.

I pushed aside the overwhelming grief and focused on the tasks at hand: picking up Eve from school, preparing dinner and getting ready for her school performance later that night. I decided not to tell her about the loss before her concert. She had a very small role, but it was still a role and tonight was about her. I didn't want to take away from that or have her worry about me. Eve was a very mature child, but still sensitive. We were very close, so I didn't want to ruin her first school performance at her new school in Melbourne.

Under the spotlight of her class performance of *Mulan*, I could see Eve's nervous little face. Even though her part was small, it meant the world to me. There she was, a small figure on a stage among all the other kids, searching the crowd for my face. Sure enough, like always, she didn't have to look for long at all. I'm always 'that' mum, the one who is waving and smiling while she's performing. I couldn't help but smile, my heart exploding with bittersweet joy. I was so proud of her but also sad about the baby I was carrying. I touched my belly softly, sending a silent message of love and an 'I'm sorry' to the little one we'd never meet.

Later, at home, I told Eve the sad news that her sibling wouldn't be joining our family. She was heartbroken, yet in true Eve style she was more worried about my wellbeing.

In this time of turmoil, our friend Georgie was a rock. I had met her through Sam when we first moved to Melbourne and she'd become a part of our very small Melbourne family. She helped navigate us through the storm, from driving me to the hospital to caring for Eve during my darkest hours. The dilation and curettage procedure at the hospital was performed under anaesthesia. By the time I arrived at the hospital I was numb to the situation. I felt emotionless. I thought perhaps I might be starting to move past this, and I felt a sense of relief.

This happened to people all the time, I thought to myself as my eyes closed, staring up at the huge surgical lights and the ceiling as a nurse gently stroked my arm, telling me I was going to be all right.

I woke up to the cries of newborn babies. This was a cruel twist, a reminder of what I had lost. I closed my eyes tightly and put my hands over my ears, trying to block out the sweet, innocent little cries that brought both happiness and sadness in that moment.

The love and care from my friends were like bright lights in a very dark time. Sam was still flying over countries and oceans on his way back to us, and kind acts from friends made it clear how important our relationships with others are when we're going through hard times, and how hard it was being away from my family.

I think I'd been on autopilot. When reality sank in, I was sucked into a downward spiral.

After I came home from the hospital, I rested on the couch and Eve was asleep in her bed. Later that night, Sam burst through the door. It had taken him over a day to get home. He hugged me so tightly, crying so much. He was crying for both of us, especially since I felt like I had no tears left.

The next few months were incredibly tough. We were heartbroken, and on top of that I was struggling with anxiety that made even stepping outside feel impossible. I longed for the simple things, like being able to go to the shop in my old tracksuit and thongs, without worrying about how I looked. But the paparazzi waiting outside for a photo made even that impossible. My sadness quickly turned into anger – at the paparazzi. And anger at myself for not realising something was wrong sooner. Rage at my own ignorance consumed me. How could I have been so unaware, so blind, to the silent tragedy unfolding within me? The heart of my unborn child had stopped beating, but I knew nothing. What did that say about me as a mother? What kind of person could be oblivious to the life inside her fading away? The guilt was suffocating, a relentless storm of self-condemnation. How could I have failed to protect, to know, to save the most precious part of me? The questions haunted me, each one a sharp jab at my soul. I was engulfed, drowning in the what-ifs and the how-could-I-haves.

I was angry at Sam for not being there when it happened. 'Why did you go? I told you *not to go!*' I found myself yelling, even though I knew him being here wouldn't have changed the outcome.

I felt guilty for taking out my frustration on Sam. He was already upset about not being there for me and was just as sad about the baby as I was. My anger only made his pain worse.

Even amid our personal turmoil, we had to keep up with public appearances, interviews and photoshoots, requiring us to mask our heartbreak. Smiling and chatting with people I'd normally enjoyed engaging with became too much. And the paparazzi who were there doing their job now became unbearable. All I wanted to do was scream at them, 'Just leave us alone! LEAVE US ALONE!' But I didn't. I kept smiling and being polite. Inside I was breaking.

This was the consequence of the life I chose when I went on *The Bachelor*. It was a harsh reminder that this path includes both the good and the bad, and now I had to face the tough parts head-on.

Eventually Sam and I were able to acknowledge that we'd been through something traumatic and had to be kind to each other and ourselves.

We were navigating our grief in different ways, a journey made even more complex by the fact that I had recently moved to Melbourne. This new beginning in a new city meant we were still in the process of discovering each other, not just as partners but as individuals sharing a life together. I found refuge in solitude, retreating inward, while Sam sought comfort in the vibrancy of the outside world, engaging more with the outside world and friends. This difference in the way we coped led to bickering, until it all came to a head with an intense argument that laid bare the depth of our pain.

In the aftermath of that heated argument, we experienced a moment of clarity. It became clear that our struggles, magnified by the challenges of me adjusting to a new city and the intricacies of living together, were not just about the loss but also about learning to live life as a couple. The realisation hit us that blaming each other for our pain was a waste of time. What mattered was the love and passion that had initially brought us together – a love that, despite everything, remained vibrant and strong.

This confrontation was a turning point, reminding us of our deep connection and the need to face our challenges together. We were still discovering each other, learning how to be partners in every sense, and now we understood that this journey required patience, understanding and mutual support. With this newfound understanding, we began to heal, finding strength in our love and in the life we were building together in Melbourne. This shared journey of healing and discovery marked a new chapter in our relationship, strengthening the idea that together, we could navigate any challenge, grow stronger, and deepen our understanding of each other in this new chapter of our lives.

CHAPTER 9

ON STRENGTH

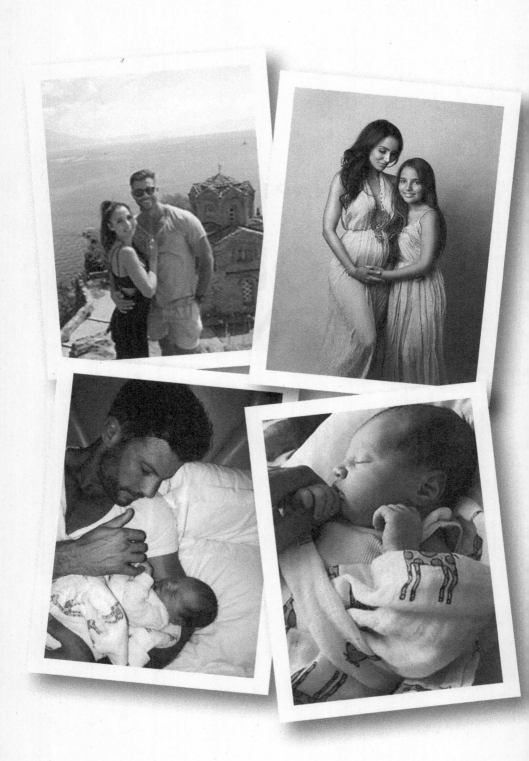

What a moment! There I was, wearing my cap and with my gown flowing behind me as I stepped onto the stage at my graduation. Nothing short of exhilarating, this day was eight years in the making – from when I started as an eager full-time student, navigating through being a single mum at university, working, with all the financial burdens, through to pausing my studies for the unexpected whirlwind of *The Bachelor*.

There was a time when the finish line seemed like a mirage, always out of reach. Yet here I stood, a testament to the power of determination and the strength of a mother who wanted more for herself and her daughter, a mum determined to show her young daughter that anything is possible. Completing the degree was an incredible relief. There had been times of doubt, and the shadow of imposter syndrome lurking at the edges. Let me tell you, though, when I crossed that stage, I realised the true measure of achievement isn't just in the relentless grind, it's in rising above every challenge, in the sheer will to continue and in the courage to chase a dream against all odds.

Yes, my university journey was a whirlwind of hustle, a balancing act of crazy proportions. But I also think of it as a beacon of hope: it's not about the perfection of our path but about embracing the journey, with all its twists and turns, and emerging victorious. I was celebrating not just a degree, but a journey of perseverance.

Standing there, during my graduation ceremony, my heart raced with anticipation. I half-expected my name to be twisted into an unrecognisable form as it was announced, and me falling flat on my face, my feet getting tangled in my cape. But in that moment I couldn't hear a thing. My nerves drowned out everything, even the possible mispronunciation of my name. There they were, my mum, dad, Eve and Sam, my pillars of strength, beaming with pride in the crowd, witnessing me stride forward to claim my hard-earned degree. This was monumental, not just for me but for all of us. My journey had been dotted with moments of uncertainty, yet here I was, proving not just to my family, but to myself, that I could see a grand project through to its end.

Even so, this achievement was bittersweet. Throughout my studies I had pictured diving headfirst into the scientific world, armed with my degree. My path seemed clear. Life, however, steered me in a new direction. Meeting Sam, moving to Melbourne and the dreams of expanding our family took precedence, shifting my priorities. My degree, a symbol of dreams and dedication, found its place on the wall, as a reminder of where I had been and a promise of possibilities yet to unfold, a cherished symbol of one journey's end and the endless possibilities that are always within in reach.

*

Sam, Eve and I stood on the brink of a new chapter in our lives, with the thrill of the unknown before us. Sam and I weren't trying to fall pregnant but at the same time we weren't trying not to fall pregnant. Planning our European wedding, we travelled, dreams in tow, to Italy's majestic Amalfi Coast. The idea to marry in

Italy was born from a blend of spontaneity and a love for 'old-school' magic. It was winter in Italy so we saw a very different Amalfi Coast – a remarkable contrast to the crowded busy streets and venues you see in the glamorous summer images. The stillness of the streets meant we could explore enchanting hotels, each offering a view more breathtaking than the last. Eventually, we found 'the one' – a venue that seemed to echo our hearts' desires, and we put down a sizeable deposit.

Returning to Melbourne, our wedding plans now in full swing, soon we found ourselves wrapped in the sweet surprise of pregnancy. Discovering I was pregnant was honestly a burst of joy, an unexpected blessing that reshaped our priorities. Expanding our family eclipsed everything else, which led to our decision to put aside wedding plans until after our baby's arrival.

This time was sacred and tender, it demanded our full presence and I wanted to be free from the pressures of organising a wedding – especially in the delicate early stages of pregnancy and after the heartache of our previous loss. We chose to hold onto this secret a while longer; even though Sam was eager to share his excitement with everyone we were waiting for the right time to ensure we were in the 'safe zone' before sharing our news with the world.

Determined to take control of my life and the growing new life inside me, I chose to step into the light on my own terms, not as a result of a long camera lens showing my belly becoming noticeably rounder. The second trimester marked a moment of relief and strength. I had control, this was my story, my joy to share, so I arranged a maternity photoshoot. This wasn't just any photoshoot; it was like a declaration of our growing family's unity and love, a moment to honour the bond between me and Eve. Recognising the delicate balance of her emotions, having been the one and only recipient of my undivided attention for nine years, it was important that Eve felt like she was a big part of this new chapter. Including Eve in the announcement and photoshoot was symbolic of her unchanging place in my heart, even as our family grew.

The photoshoot, stripped of any external pressures, was a sanctuary. It was a celebration captured by a photographer whose talent lay in portraying the essence of womanhood, making it a comfortable and empowering experience. The images from that day show a rare blend of vulnerability and strength, and they're treasures I hold dear. Despite my constant nausea, they presented a version of me that was radiant and fiercely proud. These photographs also show the beauty of motherhood, the resilience of our family and the unwavering light within us, ready to welcome the new life joining our journey.

On 8 October 2018, our lives were blessed with the arrival of our precious little baby girl, Willow, marking a new chapter as our family grew to become four. The journey to her birth was a familiar path consisting of constant Braxton Hicks contractions, which I was having from the early stages of my pregnancy, and which I also experienced during my pregnancy with Eve. Initially these contractions didn't cross the threshold into pain, they were just ever-present, tightening their grip as the months passed, forcing me to stop in my tracks, hold my belly and breathe through them until they went away. They only lasted a couple of seconds at a time but the fact that they were so regular throughout my pregnancy was what blurred the lines between normal discomfort and that of the onset of labour.

I anticipated and frankly would have loved a more dramatic sign of labour – a huge gush of my waters breaking, forming a puddle at my feet like women in the movies, the 'OMG my waters just broke!' moment, a definitive signal that meant my baby was on the way. Instead, I was oblivious to the onset of my labour. My days were filled by these contractions, a series of stops and starts that were a part of my daily life that didn't really mean much at all. I recall mentioning to Sam during a very slow walk 'Ooohhh, these damn Braxton Hicks contractions are so annoying, we're stopping every couple of minutes!' Usually most women would associate this with being in labour, but not me! I dismissed the mere mention of it from Sam with a 'No, no, don't be ridiculous, it's not labour, let's keep going.' An hour passed until I realised that they were becoming even more frequent, in fact every couple of minutes, and that perhaps Sam might be right, these contractions were more than just nothing and could be the real deal. After I monitored my contractions I decided to call the hospital and from my description of events a nurse confirmed that I was in labour. No dramatic gush of water, damn it!

Funnily enough, the urgency that typically accompanies labour wasn't occupying my mind – possibly because there was never a dramatic start to the labour. Well, for me at least. Sam wasn't so calm. He was so panicked that he wanted to throw me into the car and head straight to the hospital. I think my calmness reassured him there was no need to rush and these things take time (well, they generally do, kind of, sometimes). I was unfazed; my focus was now on a promise to Eve, a Bengal kitten. We had bought the kitten from a Sydney breeder, so we headed to Tullamarine airport because her arrival from Sydney was a priority. Our family seems to have the ability to embrace life's surprises with adaptability.

The journey to the airport was a balance between Eve's anticipation and joy for her new pet and Sam trying to mask his quiet panic. He watched me as I held my belly and breathed a little more heavily through the contractions. I was still telling him, 'It's fine, don't worry!'

The contractions, a mere background to our day so far, then began to make themselves known with more intensity, a reminder of the excruciating pain and joy this day was about to bring. But I had to fulfil one mission before surrendering to the next.

The story of Willow's birth was one of ignorance and calm amid the whirlwind of life, a story that saw us expand our family twice over, first with the arrival of a kitten, then with the birth of a beautiful baby daughter.

We made it back home and my discomfort was increasing. Eve was excited about meeting her new sister soon, but thankfully distracted by her new kitten – which she named Cinnamon, a nod to the fact she smelled like cinnamon. Eve stayed home with a friend and became acquainted with the hyperactive, excitable kitten.

We headed to the hospital and when we arrived at the birthing suite, it dawned on me that showtime was imminent – like, really now. A cocktail of excitement and terror hit me: this wasn't going to be fun. Honestly, a couple of strong margaritas would've been perfect right then. But instead I had to make do with McDonald's, which was across the road from the hospital. Yes, I made Sam walk me there to eat first. While I ate, my contractions were getting a lot stronger but I wanted to finish my Big Mac meal first. Sam was caught up in the excitement. He just couldn't wait to hold our bundle of joy.

Deciding to go au naturel for this, no epidural, just like with Eve – was I out of my mind? Had I conveniently erased the trauma from my memory? Clearly, my sanity was questionable! The reminder came fast and hard. The pain, a merciless, soul-shredding tsunami, crashed through me, with my back serving as the epicentre of a seismic event, each contraction drilling into my spine with the precision of a sadistic sculptor. And this, my friends, was the opening act – the 'magic' of childbirth was only just beginning.

Our nurses were so caring and our obstetrician's joyful, calming demeanour instantly put us at ease, but when the pain became unbearable I was so thankful to have Sam by my side, holding my hand. I crushed his hand and turned to him with every contraction from the very beginning. He never left my side. He kissed my head and talked to me quietly. Watching me in such excruciating pain and not being able to physically help meant he was being my cheerleader, which was lovely. 'You're doing great, hun', 'You've got this', 'We're nearly there'. Like I said, lovely. What more could I ask for?

The only problem was that my pain had switched into irritability – *Ummm, actually, NO, WE'RE not nearly there! I'M nearly there! You're having no part in this pain, mister!!*

The contractions were relentless, each one a wave that left me gasping, too exhausted to brace for the next. And then, the moment of truth arrived: it was time to push. By this point, I was a shadow of my former self, every ounce of energy depleted by the agony. Half-jokingly, I asked about having an epidural, knowing full well that ship had sailed, vanished over the horizon.

The push phase was a symphony of 'arghhs', each push igniting a firestorm of pain, a sensation so fierce I was convinced my body had reached its limit. 'I can't,' I whispered.

But with Sam's support and our Zen master obstetrician's guidance, I found strength I didn't know existed. Then, after what felt like a marathon through Dante's inferno, she arrived. Our daughter, our little princess, made her grand entrance, marking the end of the ordeal and the beginning of a whole new chapter. Four hours after entering through the hospital doors, there she was, proof that I, indeed, could do it – and did.

*

Reflecting on it now, I think I might have gone a tad overboard in my campaign to show Eve that my love for her hadn't just endured the newborn storm but was, in fact, doing jazz hands in the face of it. There I was, firmly planted in the chaos of our home, riding the relentless merry-go-round of feedings and nappies, and somehow deciding it was the perfect moment to audition for the role of Eve's one-woman cleaning crew. Assigning chores to Eve? Ha! As if! I was on a one-mum mission to demonstrate that the household didn't revolve solely around our latest adorable tyrant.

Let's be honest, navigating motherhood is like being on a never-ending roller coaster – part freak show, part drama series, all heart and soul. Mum 2.0 guilt had arrived.

Raising a child in Melbourne without the support of extended family was challenging. Organisational skills became crucial, a significant shift for someone like me who is very last-minute. Even simple tasks like grabbing a coffee required coordination and timing. Spontaneity was no longer an option for Sam, Eve and me.

With all our family support interstate, there was no calling in reinforcements or back-up for sick days, no quick babysitting for work tasks, and no help for brief personal breaks such as showers. Despite anticipating these challenges, especially with Eve being older and having Sam's support, the reality was more demanding than I'd ever expected. I have enormous admiration for single parents who are managing without this network. The saying that it takes a village to raise children rings incredibly true, and those navigating parenthood alone are incredibly inspiring to me. I felt so grateful to have Sam by my side.

In addition, managing the needs of a pre-teen is not easy. A lot of people might assume that having a pre-teen would be great because she could help me. Well, let me tell you something, it's not! Managing a pre-teen and a baby/toddler presents its own set of challenges. As Eve entered her pre-teen era, I quickly realised that this age group requires just as much attention and support as newborns, if not more.

They're navigating a rollercoaster of emotions, and they need a steady presence to guide them through. With a new baby in the house, there wasn't much steadiness. Finding the time for these important moments with Eve was more complicated than I had anticipated. Willow was just like Eve as a baby and her half-hour power naps meant it was difficult to be there for Eve with no distractions. Balancing the immediate and constant needs of a baby/toddler with the emotional and complex needs of a pre-teen felt like a juggling act where I was dropping the balls, one that would have been significantly easier with an extra set of hands.

Now up to Mum guilt version 2.5 – oooh, she's upgraded again and packs a stronger punch. Mum guilt is the unwelcome gift that keeps on giving. It's like carrying around a tiny, highly critical version of yourself in your pocket, constantly whispering, 'Are you sure you're doing this right?' 'Oooh, I bet she wouldn't have said that to her kids.' 'That mum is always available to play and isn't typing emails or responses with one hand while making Peppa Pig dance with the other like you do; that mum drives the teenage girls everywhere on the weekend, and picks them up, why can't you?' 'Nawww, look, they spend so much time together as teen daughter and mum, but you guys don't, every conversation is interrupted by yells of *ceće* [sister in Macedonian] or "Muuuum!" in your house.'

The pressure-cooker of parenting expectations is real, folks. Trying to keep up with school WhatsApp groups and things that are happening in class, only to have some other parents hijack the chat group with general chit-chat, so you check out and then rock up to school one day completely forgetting it was Wear Yellow to School day. What day is PE uniform day? What day is library day for which kid, when is that thing at the high school? What even was it? OMG, did we miss it again! I've lost count of the amount of times I messed up what uniform the kids were meant to be in that day, forgetting their library books, completely missing numerous high school parent catch-ups and seminars. I had zero idea what was happening at Eve's school the majority of the time. The poor kid had to work a lot of stuff out for herself and my god, do I feel like the shittiest mum in the world for that. It drains the sparkle right out of the gig, turning what should be an adventure into an episode of *Survivor: The Home Edition.*

And let's talk about my foray into 'gentle parenting'. Oh, what a joke! Turns out, my inner Zen master has a tendency to bolt after I've said something for the tenth time, leaving me to channel my inner 'psycho mum' instead. I stumbled upon this fun fact that kids are approximately 800 per cent naughtier for their mums than anyone else on the planet. I can confirm that this is true! Sam just has to give them 'the look' and they snap to attention. Meanwhile, I'm over here conducting a one-woman screamfest to get them out the door for school, providing our neighbours with their daily dose of reality TV.

Eventually I do get to the calming words, like 'Now, why did you kick your sister in the head?' And bring in the 'That was not acceptable behaviour', and 'She didn't think it was funny' conversations – but to get there I need to lose my mind first.

To those serene, calm, never-yell parents, I salute you from the chaos of my morning routine, where yelling is practically an Olympic sport and I'm not even sporty. But hey, in the grand comedy of parenting, these are the moments we'll laugh about later, right? After a good night's sleep. Or maybe a holiday without the kids! Or perhaps as we end up driving them to their next therapy session.

Living with my husband, our teenage daughter, and three little cyclones is like being the ringmaster of the world's most unpredictable circus. Picture this: one moment, you're negotiating with a teen who believes curfew is a suggestion, not a rule. The next, you're refereeing a toddler dispute over who gets to be the princess in a game where, frankly, everyone looks more like a mud monster than royalty.

Our teenage daughter is on a journey of self-discovery, which for us translates into a series of dramatic exits and slammed doors, followed by late-night heart-to-hearts about everything from friendship woes to the latest social drama. Even though you'd been asking her to talk all afternoon and she didn't want to, it's at 11.45 pm that she decides she does. Meanwhile, her younger sisters view her as a mix of rock star and strange, scary creature locked away in her room, only making an appearance to grab food, snarl at anyone in her way and return to her quarters, a combination that's as chaotic as it sounds.

Sam and I have turned into a tag-team of sorts. Our days are spent dashing between school drop-offs, 'Mum, I forgot my laptop' trips, dance classes and birthday parties with a dash of 'Did anyone feed the dog and cat?' chaos thrown in for good measure. We communicate in a series of shorthand and knowing glances that say, 'Your turn to deal with that', or 'I forgot to buy milk – again.'

Sibling rivalry in our house is like a competitive sport. The little ones argue over everything from who gets to hold the remote to who breathed on who first. Our teenager tries to stay above the fray, headphones in, then taking the side of the weaker opponent. Only all of a sudden not to be able to hear, thanks to her headphones, when asked to clean her room.

The support my husband and I offer each other is the secret to our barely surviving survival. We share the load, the laughs and the occasional meltdown, always reminding each other that this circus is ours, and we wouldn't have it any other way. Finding activities that entertain from teen to toddler is like striking gold. When we all agree on a movie or game, it's a small victory celebrated with popcorn and the kind of family bonding that makes all the chaos worthwhile.

In our household, communication is less about eloquence and more about survival. Whether it's decoding teen slang, interpreting toddler gibberish, or just trying to remember if I already asked my husband to take out the rubbish, it's all about keeping the lines open, the conversations flowing, and the laughs coming.

This circus of ours, with its high-flying acrobatics, daring feats of patience, and the occasional clown/shit-show, is the greatest show on earth. It's a life filled with love, laughter, arguments/tantrums and the kind of memories that stick with you like glitter – impossible to clean up but too sparkly to mind.

CHAPTER 10

ON MARRIAGE

During the summer of 2018 our search for the perfect wedding venue led us to the Fig Tree Restaurant in Byron Bay. After the unexpected postponement of our initial plans, Byron Bay, with its relaxed vibe and as a cherished gem in our little family getaways, was the perfect place for our big day. We wanted it to be a day bathed in the warmth of the sun, surrounded by our dearest loved ones.

The feel for our wedding would be elegance and simplicity, creating an atmosphere that was both refined and warm and inviting. I wore the most beautiful dress, my design and vision brought to life thanks to the magical hands of those at Pallas Couture. A delicate web of French lace hugged my body, long sleeves resting over my wrists and a train that followed behind were complemented by a veil that floated in the soft breeze. I felt like the epitome of timeless beauty. The meticulous fittings in Perth, which my mum, sister and daughters came along to, imbued the dress with even more significance. At the second-last fitting, the dress fitted like a glove, it was perfect. The only thing still to be finished was the hem which would rest over ivory Dior slingback heels, then my bridal look would be a dream come to life.

We decided to do the final fitting in Sydney. Flying to Sydney then bringing my dress back home was so exciting. However, when I tried it on, there was an unexpected twist – the dress hung loosely on me, as if I had suddenly shrunk. Confused and putting the weight loss down to pre-wedding stress, I faced a dilemma. The seamstresses were less than thrilled, and I was beyond embarrassed. My plan to bring the dress back to Melbourne and then to Byron Bay turned to dust. Now, the team faced the huge task of altering the hand-sewn lace dress on a tight schedule, while I scrambled to arrange for a friend to deliver the dress, crossing fingers that it would fit. A bride's last-minute panic had become my reality. In the end the dress fitted perfectly, as if it was meant to be.

Sam and I exchanged vows beneath a giant fig tree, under an arbor covered with breathtaking white blooms – hydrangeas, orchids, roses and baby's breath – creating a beautiful, romantic altar. We had champagne towers and fairy lights twinkled above long tables. It was a feast shared under the stars. Our families and friends came together, not just to celebrate a wedding, but a love story that was against all the odds.

My bridal party was a gathering of souls dear to me: my sister, two nieces, sister-in-law, cousin and a close friend. The most important role was played by Eve as my maid of honour and Willow was our precious little flower girl. My brother-in-law bravely took on the role of ring bearer and my baby brother proudly supported us as our witness.

Eve and Willow walked down the aisle side by side, hand in hand, their smiles beaming. They made their way to the sounds of the Beatles' 'Here Comes the Sun', a heartfelt nod to one of Sam's mum's favourite songs. During the ceremony Willow, in her one-year-old innocence, wandered around saying 'Mumma' and 'Dadda', occasionally getting tangled in the fabric of my veil, much to the delight of all the guests. She stole the show in such a heartwarming, sweet way. There's a unique magic in having your children be a part of your wedding – for us it added an indescribable layer of happiness, warmth and sentimentality to the celebration.

With my dad beside me, his carefree 'Ehhh' attitude in tow, making me laugh and lightening the mood to ease my nervousness, I floated down the aisle with what I hoped resembled the grace of a swan, but which I'm sure was more like the determined stomp of an off-duty Transformer. But hey, in my mind, I was the epitome of elegance. The song that played as I made my entrance was 'Never Tear Us Apart' by INXS, a song that digs deep into our love story. And there, at the altar, stood Sam, the keeper of my heart, smiling in a moment that felt as if time itself decided to take a coffee break.

The day after our wedding, we hosted a 'recovery day', which, for me, felt more like, 'Ooooh, I shouldn't have drunk so much, full-of-regret day'. My body was not onboard with the day's agenda, leading me to make an early exit, while Sam, ever the gracious host, the thought of leaving with his new wife never even entering his mind, stayed behind with our guests. There I was, cranky and nursing what I assumed was a monster hangover.

Fast-forward to our return to Melbourne, and I was practically bedridden. I didn't feel like my usual self. I was useless, which led Sam to joke, 'Maybe you're pregnant. That's about the only time you can't get out of bed.'

'Hilarious,' I retorted, not at all amused. But then panic set in. When was my last period? Amid the wedding chaos, I hadn't realised that I had missed my period. Shit!

So, I peed on a stick, and yes indeed I was pregnant. Sam and I were in pure shock, laughing, my eyes welling up, unable to register what was happening. Even more shocking, considering I was, for the lack of a better expression, shit-faced on the night of our wedding.

Plus I had been losing weight before the wedding, not gaining – a phenomenon I later learned is quite common in early pregnancy. It seemed my body had been running on sheer wedding adrenaline, only to crash and burn with morning sickness as soon as the 'I do's' were done.

Surprise, surprise, our third daughter, Charlie, had been our undercover wedding guest all along.

As for our honeymoon? Well, that ship sailed without us. The idea of battling morning, noon and night sickness in what should be a romantic getaway did not appeal to us. No, thank you. I'm holding out for the day we can jet off without nausea in tow. Here's hoping that day comes sooner rather than later, preferably before Sam and I are navigating the airport with our very own Zimmer frames.

It seems that in our love story we decided to skip the conventional chapters and dive straight into the heart of our story – our family. Our connection was pretty much instant, perhaps a result of the unique circumstances under which we met, or quite simply the undeniable pull between us. When Sam came into my life, he didn't just join me, he embraced the full package that was me and Eve, instantly creating a family unit. At the beginning of our relationship, we began to learn about each other under the watchful eyes of the public before we started to learn about each other in private. And even then, it wasn't completely private. Learning to navigate through a new relationship with an audience added layers of complexity and learning, sometimes making it very difficult to block out the outside noise but in turn making our bond stronger and more resilient.

Our relationship took the express lane, speeding quickly through the 'getting to know you' phase straight into 'let's make humans together'. This meant that we swapped romantic dinners for family feasts and weekend couple's getaways for group adventures at the local playground. Sure, there are moments when I think it would be nice to have more one-on-one time with my husband. Imagine what it would be like to have a conversation at home without being interrupted by one or all four kids at the same time?

But I wouldn't change a single bit of it for the world. On our occasional date night we get a sneak peek into who we were before becoming the tag-team, nappy-changing, story-telling mum-and-dad taxi. And that to me is like finding a little nugget of gold in a sandbox. It's thrilling and at times surreal. These rare moments remind me that beneath the parental exterior lies a vast, unexplored territory within each of us, waiting to be discovered.

That's the beauty of it. The promise of uncovering new facets of each other, not despite our whirlwind family expansion, but because of it, adds layers of excitement and mystery to our journey together. It's a chaotic and messy but ridiculously rewarding expedition and I wouldn't trade our unique path for anything. Who knew that among the mad juggling act of parenting we'd find such excitement in the little snippets of discovery. I may be tired but I'm grateful for the endless adventures of learning, laughing and growing together, one unexpected revelation at a time.

*

There were a few challenges here and there, but overall, being pregnant with a pre-teen daughter had been fine. Fast-forward to pregnancy with a teenager and a toddler, well ... this took me into an entirely new realm.

With my first pregnancy during Eve's pre-teen years, life was busy with school drop-offs, homework and after-school activities, but there were still those precious moments of calm while she was at school. Even after school she was old enough to understand that Mummy needed some rest. There were hours when I could catch my breath, put my feet up and wallow in self-pity about my all-day sickness misery – a constant battle with nausea that never seemed to end, offering no relief, morning, day or night.

The nausea medication wasn't working and the only escape from feeling ill was when I'd stuff my face with some serious carbs like pasta or bread. This gave me short-lived relief – fifteen minutes to be exact. I was lucky enough during that time to find pockets of rest, moments to just lie down and muster up some energy.

However, the experience of being pregnant while juggling the needs of a teenager and a toddler was a whole different scenario. The idea of resting, of simply sitting down and taking a moment for myself, became a fantasy. From the moment the day started, it was a hurricane of activity: making snacks, visiting parks, engaging in play – all while feeling like I was barely hanging on. The relentless pace of motherhood intensified by pregnancy nausea turned every day into a test of stamina, leaving the luxury of 'putting your feet up' as a fond but distant memory.

During this pregnancy, Sam became the ultimate sidekick. He was there to help me with the simplest tasks, like putting on my shoes when my belly and I reached a mutual agreement to no longer see my feet. He'd help roll me off the bed and couch with all the grace of a log-rolling competition, and matched my pace to a slow shuffle whenever those Braxton Hicks contractions decided to throw a surprise party. Our walks often turned into impromptu standstills, while we patiently waited for the sensation to return in my right leg.

My face was covered with melasma (brown patches), a recurring souvenir from each pregnancy, and my feet had transformed to a size where shoes were no longer an option. Yet Sam never missed a beat in reminding me of my beauty and his love for me. Despite it all, Sam's constant reassurances of beauty and love were soothing, making the challenging moments warmer and lighter. It's funny how, amid pregnancy's less glamorous side, his words and actions managed to make everything feel just a bit more special.

Charlie was born in the winter of 2019 – past her due date, fashionably late, an early sign of her love of fashion, her stubbornness and her 'I play by my own rules' personality that was to come. This time around, I opted for an epidural, a change from my all-natural experiences with Eve and Willow. Having already experienced the magic – cough, cough – of natural childbirth twice, I was curious about the epidural hype. Well, my epidural experience was nothing short of fantastic, despite the initial hiccup when the needle had to be repositioned in my back twice while Sam looked on, as pale as a ghost. It was a walk in the park compared with my last two experiences.

Before the epidural my contractions were uncomfortable, but I wouldn't say painful. Once the epidural took effect, I was just sitting back on that maternity ward bed, relaxing, casually asking Sam to go grab me a snack from the cafeteria. While Sam went on his mission, I drifted off for an itty-bitty nap, and when he returned, the midwife, looking curious and confused, asked if I had been feeling any pain.

I replied, 'Nah, just a bit of pressure, but I'm fine,' as I started to eat the muffin Sam had brought me.

Soon, a second midwife joined the first. 'Ok, you're crowning, DON'T PUSH, we're getting the doctor!'

I figured this would be as good a time as any to put down the muffin. The Zen master obstetrician appeared. And within twelve minutes I was holding our gorgeous little Charlie Bear in my arms! With a full head of black hair and the biggest eyes I'd ever seen, she was beautiful.

'WOW, I can have babies every year if this is what it's like having them with an epidural,' I joked.

Luckily for us, my mum had flown across from Perth a couple of days earlier and stayed for two weeks to help us adjust to being a family of five.

The early newborn days were a blur, and just as I started to come out from the haze, the world stopped. The Covid pandemic arrived in Australia, closing borders and locking down states.

CHAPTER 11

ON LOSS

Losing my maternal grandparents was a heart-breaking experience, but what deepened the sadness was witnessing my mum's grief. Her pain was palpable, facing the loss of her parents who had remained in North Macedonia while we lived in Australia, unable to see them as often as she would have liked and not being with them in their final moments. When my dedo, Milan, a funny and very witty hardworking man. passed away unexpectedly at sixty, I was just thirteen. The geographical distance strangely cushioned the blow for me. It almost seemed as if he was still alive, just far away. Many years later, my baba, Neda, a physically and mentally strong yet nurturing woman passed away at eighty-nine. The reality was softened by the few precious visits we made to Macedonia, allowing us to cherish these moments with her. Though each loss was deeply felt, the physical distance allowed me to dig my head in the sand and continue as if it never happened. Which, years down the track, unknowing at the time, I would experience yet again.

From the day I was born my paternal grandparents were a constant presence in our lives. They lived with us in our family home in Perth. Whenever we woke, whenever we went to bed, they were there, just as our parents were. When the time came and we moved to a new house (we didn't go far – just twenty-seven doors down on the same street), my grandparents chose to stay in our original family home, finding comfort in its familiarity.

As the seasons of my life changed, from the innocence of childhood to the trials of adulthood, the breakdown of my first marriage and the joyous arrival of my gorgeous daughter Eve, my grandparents were there for all of it. No matter what happened they were always close by. When I was young my dedo, Trifun, would play chasey and cops and robbers with me when nobody else would; he helped me make cubby houses – I loved making cubby houses when it was raining outside. We'd use a big clear plastic sheet and I'd watch the rain fall above. Nika, my baba, was there to bring the snacks and laugh and tell him he was as childish as his grandchildren. I have the fondest memories of life with my grandparents as a child, and as an adult. Even when I had to try and explain to them, 'Nope! No, no, nooo, Baba, I don't need my jeans fixed, they're meant to have rips in them!' This particular conversation went around in circles for a while – she just didn't understand why you would buy jeans that were already ripped.

When Eve and I moved to Melbourne, nothing hit harder than being away from my family. I missed them deeply and the fact that my grandparents were growing older was really tough. The daily, impromptu visits were no longer – suddenly, they were thousands of miles away. I really tried to bridge that gap, planning visits whenever I could to soak up those precious moments, especially because they missed Eve so much. They had seen her every day of her life until the day we left for Melbourne. Then the pandemic hit, and with it, lockdowns. The trips back home were now off the table.

In 2020, a familiar routine took an unexpected turn. My baba was taken to hospital. It wasn't something that usually worried us too much – her trips to the hospital for fluid on her lungs had become somewhat routine. A few days of care, and she'd be back home, almost as sprightly as ever considering her age. But this time, things didn't go as planned. When she tried to call a nurse for assistance and got no response, Baba decided to take matters into her own hands. Unfortunately, her strength wasn't what it needed to be, and she took a fall, hitting her head. It was a moment that reminded us all how quickly circumstances can change. Following my baba's fall, the doctors discovered bleeding on her brain. Due to her age and other factors, surgery wasn't an option, leaving us with very few ways to help her. She couldn't return home; the brain injury had robbed her of the ability to stand or walk. The medical team advised that she be moved to a care facility where she could receive the constant attention and supervision she now required. It was an agonising choice for my parents to face, but they made the decision out of necessity.

Baba struggled with the change. Confusion and anger clouded her understanding of why she couldn't return to the comfort of her home, and beside Dedo.

The situation was further complicated by the strict Covid restrictions, which limited visits to two hours a day. Dedo could barely see her, a cruel twist to their long life together. It was a heart-wrenching period, marked by frustration and helplessness, as the pandemic's restrictions intensified the emotional toll on our family.

Doing their best to bridge the distance, my family would FaceTime me during their visits to the hospital. Some days, Baba would be her usual self, engaging and present. But on other days, it was a different story. She'd have this distant, starry-eyed look, gazing into the unknown, lost to the moment. Watching her drift between these states, separated by screens and miles, was difficult.

Just days before Willow's and my birthday in October 2020, my baba passed away. My dad was by her side. Knowing she wasn't alone in her final moments was comforting, but it couldn't ease the sadness and loss I felt. I received the news on the day we moved to Mount Martha on the Mornington Peninsula. Amid the chaos of packing and anticipation of new beginnings, this news gave me a sharp jolt of reality.

On the way to our new home, my phone buzzed with a text. Caught up in excitement of our arrival, I chose not to stop and read it immediately. It was only after parking that I checked my phone, finding a message from a friend back in Perth expressing condolences for my grandmother's passing. Confused, I immediately called my parents.

'What the hell is going on? Why am I receiving messages about Baba?' I demanded. My mum gently explained that she had passed away overnight. They had intended to tell me themselves, but knew I was on the road and didn't want to risk upsetting me while I was driving with my daughters. 'We were waiting for you to arrive safely in Mount Martha before we called,' Mum said. But the news had reached me through my friend's message first, leaving me to deal with the loss in the middle of the stress and chaos of moving.

The news of Baba's passing hit us all like a tonne of bricks, leaving us in a state of shock and deep sorrow. It was hard to grasp the fact that my baba was gone. Such a huge part of my life was truly gone. The fact that I hadn't had the chance to say goodbye added to the unreality, making it all so difficult to accept. The distance was like a barrier, and I bitterly regretted it.

My heart broke for Dedo, who was devastated beyond words. The loss left him shattered and he sank into a depression. It was heart-wrenching to speak to him; he was so lost without Baba. They had been together for so many years. My dad stayed with Dedo around the clock, making sure he wasn't alone through the darkest of his days.

My dedo was vibrant and joyous, always laughing, and he had the ability to befriend anyone he crossed paths with. Conversations with his broken English flowed effortlessly – he had such a social nature and a love for engaging with others. His days often involved visits with friends and neighbours, exchanging stories and veggies and fruit from their gardens.

On one particular day, my dad was working from Dedo's house, ensuring my granddad took his medication on time. Dedo's habit of briefly stepping out was well known, so initially my dad wasn't concerned that he wasn't home. Then as time ticked by and Dedo hadn't returned, Dad started to worry and went to look around the backyard in case he was out there tinkering with something, as he liked to do. Dad then walked from the back of the house, tracing Dedo's potential steps toward the front yard. That's when the unthinkable happened. He found Dedo, face-down on the lawn, his hands resting straight down beside him.

It was November, six weeks after my grandmother's passing. It felt like the timing was more than coincidental, that Dedo had succumbed to his broken heart. The depth of his and Baba's bond was such that living without her would have seemed unbearable for him.

I found out about Dedo passing away under less-than-ideal circumstances, adding a surreal layer to an already devastating situation. In the middle of everything, my dad unknowingly dialled my number and left a voicemail – he never left voicemails. And I never listen to voicemails. I missed the call and tried to call back. No one answered. The voicemail had me curious, so I listened ... only to be met with the heart-wrenching sounds of a scene unfolding in the background. My dad was speaking with paramedics who were trying to revive Dedo. The gravity of the situation, the urgency in their voices and the reality of what was happening hit me all at once – through a mistakenly made phone call. Dad was completely unaware.

I immediately called my mum to ask her if what I had just heard was true. She confirmed the worst, saying, 'Yes, they're outside trying to revive him, and it doesn't seem good.'

A detail, a bag of lemons lying next to him, painted a vivid picture of his final moments – visiting a neighbour, sharing, and exchanging the fruits of their gardens. The position of his hands, not positioned to break his fall, suggested that he died suddenly. While the shock of losing him so abruptly was hard to bear, there was a small comfort in knowing he likely didn't suffer in his final moments. Dedo's last act, characterised by his love of sharing and connecting, perfectly summarised the essence of who he was – a person always looking to bring a little bit of light and warmth into the lives of those around him.

Witnessing both his parents pass away in less than two months was a gut-wrenching and heartbreaking experience for my dad. We sought comfort in the thought that Baba and Dedo were reunited, likely laughing and bickering, just as they always had. The idea that they would never have to feel the loneliness of being apart again was bittersweet.

Unfortunately, lockdowns added yet another layer of distress, because I was unable to attend my grandparents' funerals. Being unable to stand beside my dad, mum, siblings and the rest of our family during those final moments of farewell was heartbreakingly difficult.

Eve was deeply shaken by the deaths of both her great-grandparents. My grandparents had been a second set of grandparents to her. The distance made it challenging for us to process our loss fully; it felt as though we were deprived of a proper chance to mourn. To this day, stepping inside their home remains beyond us. Despite returning to Perth several times since they passed away and visiting their graves, we haven't been able to walk into their house. I've managed to leave a flower from the garden where my grandad was found, a small tribute, but entering the house is a step I find too painful to take. Everything inside remaining untouched in my memory means I can maintain the illusion that they're still with us. Baba in the kitchen cooking and watching *The Bold and the Beautiful*, and Dedo scribbling notes and new English phrases or words that he'd heard that day. He was always teaching himself more English words until the very end. Stepping inside their home would shatter that illusion, confronting me with the reality – a reality I'm not sure I'm prepared to face. They're no longer here and accepting that feels like saying goodbye for the final time.

CHAPTER 12

ON SURVIVAL

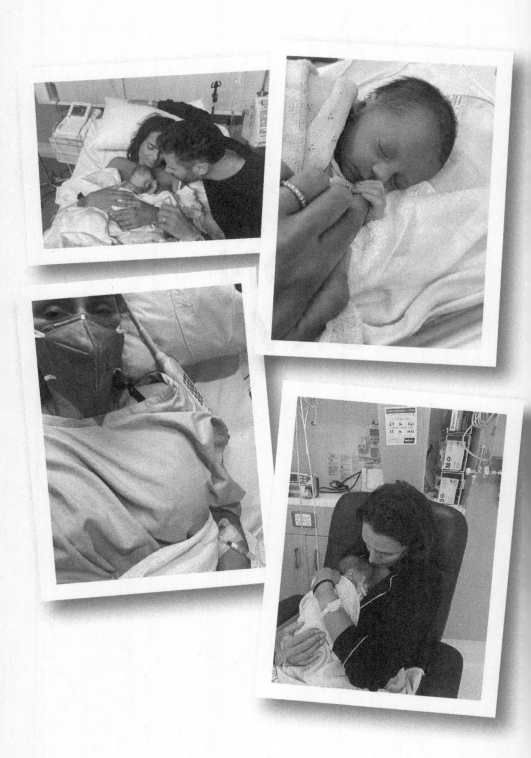

From the moment I found out I was pregnant with Harper in 2021, I was very, very sick. I had felt unwell in my other pregnancies, but this time it was significantly worse than any of those put together. I was suffering from extreme fatigue and was constantly nauseous. My hormone levels resembled those of someone carrying multiple babies, explaining the severity of my nausea. I couldn't get up. I just didn't feel right.

I would battle through each day. I struggled to wake in the mornings and I'd push my way through the morning before-school chaos. Charlie loved to be super-active, which required energy and stamina I could no longer provide, so we decided to enrol her in some activities to give her stimulation. We booked her into an early learning centre a couple of days a week. She loved learning and being active, and it allowed me to get a couple of hours' break.

Even so, there was no reprieve for me. I felt so weak all the time and had to set my alarm to make sure I started to hype myself up to pick up the girls from school. I can't even begin to express the way I felt. I would cry uncontrollably because I didn't know how I was going to walk eight minutes up the road to pick them up, and as I've said before I don't cry easily. My legs felt too weak to carry my body and I felt guilty putting pressure on Sam, who was busy at work – and I knew what his work days were like.

I had no choice but to put on a brave face and make the short but excruciating walk, telling myself the entire time that I was okay, that I could do this, and praying that I didn't pass out on the way. I had never felt anything like this before. Because I felt so sick, the doctors put me on a steroid that wasn't harmful to the baby but would be strong enough to ease my sickness as the standard pregnancy nausea prescriptions weren't working in the slightest.

Already feeling hideous physically and close to mentally defeated, the steroid meant my skin broke out in what looked like acne all over my face, and if you know anything about steroid medications, they are known to give the user something called 'moonface'. They make your face swell so it looks like a full moon, and sure enough that's what I looked like.

In the amniotic fluid test, there were some genetic mutations and abnormalities in my placenta. We didn't know if there was a mutation in a gene within Harper, or if it was just within the cells of my placenta. In doing the test – and finding out it was just the placenta – the doctors discovered something else that wasn't quite right.

I was five months' pregnant and we didn't know if Harper was going to be okay. It was terrifying. We didn't know if the next set of genetic testing was going to provide us with even more sinister information which might force us to make an unthinkable decision. The whole process of doing the genetic testing and then waiting weeks on end for the results was excruciating.

Sam and I had to get tested and so did my parents. It was a very stressful waiting game – on top of me already feeling like complete crap 24/7. Before this downward spiral with all the testing, we had organised a belated housewarming party at our house, which I was now dreading. I wanted to cancel the entire thing. I couldn't think of anything worse. But Sam, ever the optimist, insisted we stay positive and move forward with it. In a way he was right, but having to pretend to everyone (except my closest girlfriends) that everything was fine and dandy aside from the all-day sickness was very hard. Our guests were enjoying themselves and I just wanted to go to my room, curl up in a ball and cry both from how sick I felt and the unknown factors surrounding my pregnancy.

Thanks to my lazy placenta not doing its job of ensuring Harper was receiving everything she needed to grow, she had to be monitored regularly for her size. She was a little bit on the smaller side.

Towards the last few months of my pregnancy I would have loved nothing more than to lie in bed and rest – like most doctors tell you to – but with three kids at home that wasn't an option. I just had to power on. I did what I had to do: cried, vented, then just got on with it.

Five to six weeks before Harper was due, I started getting uncontrollably itchy all over my body, not just on my tummy. I immediately suspected this had something to do with my liver. A week later (a month before Harper was due) I was on the couch watching a trashy show on TV while the rest of the house was fast asleep. I started to feel really cold. The fireplace was on and I had a big blanket on me, but I was still cold.

Sam runs hot so he's always radiating heat at night and I knew if I jumped into bed I'd warm up instantly next to him. But for the first time ever, it didn't work. By now I was shaking so much that I woke Sam up, and he asked if I was okay. 'Yeah, I'm just really cold, it's cold in here.'

'No, it's not,' he told me.

'It is. It's freezing,' I replied through chattering teeth.

Sam turned the heater up and put blanket after blanket on me. He was hugging me and rubbing me, trying anything to get me warm, but it wasn't working.

'This doesn't seem right to me,' Sam said.

'I'm just cold,' I said, adamant that it was nothing serious.

Sam said he wanted to take me to the hospital, but I was stubbornly refusing because I didn't feel any more ill than I had every other day of my pregnancy. I just felt cold. 'It's Melbourne, it's cold,' I said. I told him I had an appointment the next morning with my obstetrician so if I wasn't feeling well when I woke up I'd let him know. Eventually, I tired myself shaking to sleep, and when I woke up in the morning, I felt completely fine.

'Are you sure you're okay? You were really shaking last night,' Sam said.

'I'm completely fine,' I said as I slowly sat up in bed. When I went to stand up, I felt a small amount of water. I didn't know if my waters had broken, or if my bladder was just shot from having had three kids and one on the way. I told Sam and he wanted to call the doctor and the hospital. I said we'd just let the obstetrician know when we got to our appointment.

It didn't seem like I was in active labour. I was sure it was just the Braxton Hicks contractions popping up as they always did, so I wasn't worried. I thought I might have just peed myself.

We went to the doctor's appointment. My previous obstetrician was no longer delivering babies and had recommended we see his colleague who was working in the same rooms. So far the new obstetrician had been incredibly understanding and also made us feel at ease. I let him know about what happened in bed that morning. I intentionally didn't mention the night before because I felt it was ridiculous. Then big-mouth Sam dobbed me in. He explained what happened the night before. I could see the obstetrician thinking. Meanwhile, I was downplaying the entire thing, insisting I had just been cold, nothing more serious than that. He was piecing things together: the itchiness, the coldness, the baby being on the small side. After examining me, the doctor confirmed my waters had broken and said that I'd have to go straight up to the birthing suite. He told me I was in labour; I didn't even know. Again!

In the birthing suite, I decided to have an epidural because my experience with Charlie had been such a positive one that I wanted it again. This time, I thought I'd get it in nice and early before I felt any labour pain. I was excited about getting the epidural and looking forward to a relatively pain-free birth, just like it was with Charlie.

After the needle went into my spine, they said it would take fifteen minutes to take effect and a couple of hours before anything would start to happen. Before the fifteen minutes were up, the doctor examined me and monitored Harper. He couldn't get a good reading on her. I was nowhere near fully dilated, and my hind waters were still intact, so to speed things along he popped the waters, and then asked me to lie on my side as they needed me in a different position to be able to monitor Harper's heartbeat and vital signs. As I was rolling onto my side before the epidural had even taken kicked in, the pain hit me with the full force of Dante's inferno yet again. It was horrendous – within a second it went from mild discomfort to the most unbearable, excruciating pain I have ever experienced. It went from a two to an eleven level of pain instantly – no warning, no lead-up, just BAM! It was there. I had to start pushing straightaway. My body was fast-tracking Harper's birth.

Four minutes, that was it. I was lying on my side, yelling, screaming and swearing for four minutes. The pain was so incredibly unbearable. It wasn't as if this was my first rodeo and I didn't know what to expect, but you normally get a warm-up in preparation for the crescendo. There was none of that it. I think I only pushed twice.

'She's here!' Sam called out, elated.

'Who's here?' I asked, a little dazed and confused and in shock. It was all so quick. I didn't have time to think or react. And the epidural didn't have time to work. 'Our little girl is here,' he said.

Harper didn't immediately cry and those few seconds of silence felt like an eternity. Sam and I just looked at each other. Our hearts started to sink, but before we could say anything she let out the sweetest cry, music to our ears. My heart was exploding with so much love for our little baby. I recall the nurses running around, getting things prepared for her. No one had been ready for her lightning-fast arrival.

They placed Harper in my arms – she was so small and so gorgeous. I can't even express the happiness I felt in that moment. I couldn't stop staring at her and kissing her as she lay on my chest. As I was holding my angel in my arms, I suddenly started to feel a little cold. I asked Sammy to put a blanket on us. I didn't think much of it at first. But then I started shivering and I said to Sam, 'I can't stop shaking. I'm so cold.'

Sam looked at me, realised something wasn't right and told the nurses. They said that it was probably just the adrenaline running through me and that this can happen after giving birth.

Luckily, my obstetrician was still in the room asking to have my placenta tested and sent to the lab.

'This is what happened last night,' Sam explained to him. And with one look at me, he immediately asked Sam take Harper from me. He knew something was very wrong. I'm vague about what happened next. Sam told me there was a lot of running around in the room and low conversations among the doctors and midwives. People were in and out. By this time my shaking had become uncontrollable. I couldn't keep my body still – it was like I was convulsing but I was still conscious. And I couldn't do anything to stop it.

The nurses were trying to find a vein so they can put in a cannula, but my arms were shaking too much. They eventually managed to hold an arm down and find a vein and after this, everything was a little hazy. I recall a nurse trying to keep me awake, telling me, 'No, no, don't close your eyes, look at me, don't close your eyes.'

It was so hard keeping my eyes open. My doctor suspected I had sepsis and started giving me the appropriate antibiotics immediately. I wanted to know how Harper was. 'Is she okay? Where is she?' They told us they needed to take her to the special-care unit but that she was okay and in good hands.

I recall I'd asked to give her a little kiss before they took her away and asked Sam to go with her and make sure everything was all right. I was scared for her. I wanted to be with her. I had just given birth and all I wanted to do was hold my baby and now she was being taken away. Then we received another blow as ambulance officers entered the birthing suite. I was confused.

'We need to transfer you to another hospital, Harper will need to stay here,' they said. My heart was shattering.

I was immediately transferred to the ICU of the other hospital which, luckily for Sam, was just around the corner. He was torn between being with me and being with Harper, but I insisted he stay with our baby and make sure she was okay.

I stayed in hospital for days. I was being monitored around the clock. I was given antibiotics intravenously every few hours as well as painkillers, but I was in so much pain. It felt like I was being repeatedly stabbed in my lower back.

The midwives would come across to my hospital to collect colostrum and breast milk from me to take back to Harper. I was grateful for how attentive and dedicated they were in giving Harper what she needed in those first few days of her life.

The nurses came multiple times a day, and the only time I saw Harper was via FaceTime. Sam was with her, and he would FaceTime me as much as he could. I was grateful he was there with her. Her heart and breathing were also being monitored closely as there may have been some weakness in her cardiac muscle, and she was being given antibiotics for infection. It was so hard not being with her and knowing that she wasn't well. She was tiny – she was a month premature, and she hadn't been getting the nutrients she needed from my placenta.

I just wanted to hold her. I'd only had a chance to cuddle her for twenty minutes before she was taken away, and then I was taken away. Nothing could have prepared me for the pain of being separated.

I was more afraid about what was happening to Harper than what was happening to me. I didn't realise how sick I had been until a month or so later. At the time, though, I didn't know any of that. My primary concern was getting out of ICU and back to Harper.

The doctors would ask me how I felt. 'I'm fine, can I leave now?' I kept saying.

If I had known how sick I was, I might have gone down a dark rabbit hole. I would have started to worry about dying and leaving my kids without a mother. I'm sure I would have worried myself sick. Or sicker. I think the fact that I was unaware – or so focused on getting better and out of the ICU – was a blessing in disguise.

Sam held it together. He played it cool, never showing a sign that he was really worried about both me and Harper. Whenever he came to my hospital room, I'd tell him, 'Just go and make sure Harper is okay.'

Sam was back and forth between hospitals day and night. My close friend Georgie was there to help with the girls. Once we told my parents Harper and I were in hospital and unwell they flew across immediately to help. I missed my other three girls dearly but I knew they were being looked after by close family and friends, which helped put my mind at ease and allowed me to focus on Harper and getting better.

While in the ICU I was awake, but because I was on so many painkillers and felt so weak and drowsy I was in and out of awareness the whole time. Eve came to visit me in the ICU with a couple of friends, 'Don't you remember, Mum? We got kicked out because there were too many of us,' she told me later. I didn't remember.

Eve still hadn't met her youngest baby sister; none of the girls had. Only parents could enter the special-care unit. I do recall having another episode of the violent shaking while the doctors were present with me in the ICU – I crazily thought if I could fight these shakes, get control of my body, I would be okay and could leave and get back to Harper. I'm not sure how I thought this would happen considering the doctors and nurses could see me physically shaking. Nevertheless, I was determined to try so I could get the hell out of there as soon as possible. I needed to be with my baby.

Sam continued to jump from one hospital to the other to see us both, but I kept telling him his time was better spent with Harper. I remember asking the doctors and nurses when I could go home every time they entered my room. There was always a group of doctors coming in and discussing things, but I was too out of it on painkillers to really understand what was happening or what was being said. All I knew and cared about was leaving.

After a couple of episodes and what seemed like litres of intravenous antibiotic and painkiller cocktails, the day came when I was well enough to be transferred back to Harper's hospital. I was beyond happy, I was finally going to be together with my precious little baby. Walking through the special-care unit towards my baby, I felt a surge of emotions spilling out of me. I remember her being small, but she was so much smaller than I'd expected.

My heart was full and exploding with happiness and love, but at the same time it ached and broke seeing so many tubes all over her tiny little frame. I sat down and she was gently handed to me. I couldn't stop crying. I could finally hold her in my arms.

I was so happy to be in the maternity hospital with Harper. I was by her side every chance I could get, only breaking away when I had to return to my room and sit for the next round of IV antibiotics or to see my other three girls and family. That's when I started to get hints of just how serious my condition had been.

The doctors and nurses on the ward were surprised to see me back so soon.

'What are you doing back?' they said. 'We didn't think we'd see you back so soon! You weren't well at all! We were all really worried about you!'

They said this over and over again, but I'd laugh it off and say, 'Oh, I'm fine.'

My mum and dad recall being told by my doctor that they were all worried about losing me, that I was very lucky.

I was very lucky indeed. Harper and I both were because we had such an incredibly quick-thinking doctor with a deep knowledge of obstetrics and illness relating to childbirth. His ability to listen and note concerns made by his patients allowed him to do what he does best. I am forever grateful to him for ensuring Harper and I eventually went home together. I had no idea that anybody thought my life was in danger. I thought they were being a bit dramatic, and I just was a little unwell. I had no idea that it was a life-or-death situation.

After so many antibiotics – IV and oral – I was finally allowed to go home. You'd think I'd be happy but I was torn. I was happy to be home with my family, but devastated to leave little Harper. She wasn't going anywhere anytime soon. She would need to remain in special care for at least another month. I didn't want to leave her. I hated the thought of it. I cried and I didn't want to say goodbye. 'What if something happens and I'm not there?' I worried.

For the next month my days were spent travelling back and forth from the hospital. I'd spend as much of my day as I could at the hospital. I'd go there to express and leave milk for Harper and hold her in my arms for hours on end, staring at her little face. In the beginning she was tube-fed with the occasional attempt at bottle feeding. As she grew stronger we alternated tube and bottle feeding. She still needed to get stronger and bigger before we moved onto her breastfeeding as well. Because she was still small and weak, breastfeeding would only result in her exerting too much energy and losing weight.

I'd go home and see my three other daughters for a very short amount of time. I felt like I was constantly expressing milk, attached to a machine that ironically sounded like a cow mooing. My girls still weren't allowed to visit Harper. I'd go back to the hospital to do the night shift until the nurses would basically kick me out so I could go home to get some sleep.

It hurt having to leave Harper in hospital, but knowing the nurses were taking such good care of her eased my mind for the few hours I couldn't be with her. I'd be back the next day doing exactly the same thing. I was running on adrenaline.

It was a tug of war. When I was at home, I was worried about Harper. When I was with Harper, I was worried about the other girls. I would cry on my way home from the hospital, and again on my way to the hospital. I missed the other girls like crazy and felt guilty for not being able to see them or really spend much time with them.

It was awful seeing Harper in hospital. She was tiny and her hands were so skinny. She had no muscle on her. She was skin and bone. She had tubes in her nose and she would fling her arms around and rip the cannulas from her hands. It was a challenge keeping them in. Watching the paediatricians putting them back in was heart-wrenching – looking for such a fine vein in her tiny little arms wasn't easy. They had to hold her arms very tightly, and she would scream and cry. The screams were haunting. They weren't little baby cries; they were a screams of pain and terror.

She would stare at me as if to beg, 'Mum, make it stop.' The look in her eyes was so helpless. It cut straight through me. I swear I could feel her pain.

She would stop crying relatively quickly after the process was over. As brutal as it was watching, I wanted to be there for those moments to make sure that she was okay and she could see me, so she knew Mummy was right there with her.

Harper's sisters didn't meet her until she was a month old. Up until that point, Sam and I were the only ones who had held her. None of our family got to see her until then.

It was a rough start to life, but Harper was a fighter. There's a photo of her in Sam's arms when she was eight days old. He's cradling her tiny body in his hand against his chest and kissing her forehead. It was heartbreaking for us to see her like this, but things could have been worse. This was a mere blip in our lives in comparison to what some families go through with their newborns, having been witness to this while we were in hospital. Harper was completely fine in comparison. My heart would not only break for my little baby but for all the other little babies in the hospital units struggling with their own conditions and situations.

We were lucky. I even feel guilty writing about our experience in this book knowing that there are others in the world in worse situations, but I had to keep reminding myself this was my/our story and I'm just sharing it.

Witnessing the first encounter between Harper and her three sisters was nothing short of magical. It was a moment that as a parent I cherish so deeply – the looks on their faces when they first laid eyes on their newest little (and I mean itty-bitty) family member for the first time. My three older daughters had been eagerly awaiting the day that they could meet their baby sister in person, a moment that, until then, must have seemed like a distant dream to them.

Despite our FaceTime calls and the photos we shared, nothing could truly prepare Eve for the reality of meeting Harper. The day we brought her home, Eve was genuinely astonished by how tiny she was. Willow and Charlie thought Harper was the cutest and best addition to their doll collection as their clothes would most definitely fit. Some would even be too big for her. Needless to say, this situation had to be carefully monitored at all times, with us repeatedly explaining, 'She's not a doll!'

Harper was finally with us, completing our family. We were now a family of six with four beautiful daughters, each unique and loved with our entire beings. Our hearts overflowed with love and gratitude for these precious moments and the incredible journey ahead as a fuller, even more chaotic and at times dysfunctional family.

CHAPTER 13

ON HAVING A BEAUTIFUL MIND

I find it difficult to stay on topic and explain something in a linear, organised way. My mind jumps from one idea to the next with zero warning. In conversations I dip and dive through subjects and situations, leaving people feeling dizzy. All this, compliments of my rapid thought processing.

Trying to write at the same speed at which the narrator in my head is talking is hard work. School assignments meant messy handwriting, gaps in sentences and jumping from topic to topic, especially if we had one hour to complete an English assessment in class. Hence writing this book has been nothing short of a huge challenge.

So how and when was I diagnosed with ADHD? I was diagnosed at the age of forty-one, not long after Eve was first diagnosed. When Eve was in high school, she was assessed for ADHD. We had to do a series of tests and fill out questionnaires. The psychiatrist and psychologist gave us lots of information and recommended videos to watch on YouTube, to educate us as parents so we had greater awareness. As we explored the ADHD traits, Sam and Eve gave me those unmistakable 'Oh my god, that's you!' looks. It was like the videos were custom-made messages from the cosmos, telling the story of my life: a brain that dances to its own beat, an attention span that could lose a race to a distracted kitten and a habit of diving into projects with a firework's burst of excitement, only to leave them in the dust when the next shiny thing caught my eye. Yet, when something truly captured my interest, my focus would be razor-sharp, cutting through distractions with intensity.

I knew my brain worked in different ways to the people around me. I would listen to my teachers talking and desperately try to retain the information. Despite all my efforts, it was a struggle. The second I'd walk out of the classroom was the second the information walked out of my mind. This was typically the case with topics that weren't engaging or of much interest to me. On the flipside, give me a visual representation of what was being said – something more engaging, something in which I have a genuine interest – then it's a completely different story. Having a visual cue allowed me to create a mental picture that was easier for me to retain than purely verbal or textual information.

I could cram for an exam and feel confident walking into the room, but if one little thing distracted me it would derail everything. Even if I knew the answers, I couldn't get them out if I couldn't focus. That had been torture for me in school, but I didn't let it put me off doing my degree. If only I'd known then why I was the way I was.

An ADHD brain is like your phone when you've got a million apps open at once. Every app is beeping, popping up notifications, tempting you with something interesting, kind of like your brain refusing to stick to just one thought. Unlike someone who can just focus on one app at a time, if you have ADHD, your brain is flipping through ideas and to-dos like someone channel surfing at warp speed. This ability to bounce around actually makes you super creative and quick at connecting the dots, even in ways others might not see.

It's like your brain is the ultimate multitasker, always ready to jump on a new idea or solve problems on the fly, turning the chaos of those open apps into your superpower.

There's this unfair misconception about people with ADHD, making it seem like we're not as intelligent or capable as others. That's just not true. Having ADHD doesn't mean you're lazy or not smart; it just means you think differently from the conventional way. ADHD doesn't fit neatly into the small box of tests and the usual measures of intelligence, such as standardised testing. These don't allow for creative thinking, for the ability to solve problems and the unique viewpoints of people with ADHD. The real issue isn't with the people themselves but with a system that values everyone thinking in the same way over acknowledging different ways of thinking. It's a system that doesn't nurture creativity.

Think of ADHD like being given a set of painter's brushes instead of the standard HB pencil everyone else is using. At first glance, it might seem challenging to write an essay with a brush that's meant for painting. But once you learn how to use it, you realise you can create vibrant pictures, broad strokes, and detailed scenes that pencils can't easily replicate. You're not just conveying ideas; you're painting thoughts, emotions, and solutions in a way that's uniquely yours.

The issue isn't about us as individuals; it's about a system that favours fitting in over celebrating the unique ways we all think. ADHD can be likened to a superpower and when harnessed effectively, can lead to creative thinking and resilience. The key is to understand and use these unique abilities. Learning to navigate ADHD involves recognising your strengths and finding strategies that align with them – turning obstacles into assets.

As a woman in my early forties juggling the vibrant chaos of life with four girls (one with ADHD), a husband, and my own ADHD, I've come to realise that my craving organisation isn't just a preference, it's my lifeline. Living with ADHD means my brain is often a tornado of thoughts, ideas and distractions. Because of this internal commotion, having a neat and orderly space isn't just nice to have – it's essential.

For me, external clutter is more than an eyesore; it's a direct line to feeling overwhelmed and unfocused.

A tidy environment is soothing to my frantic mind, reducing the sensory overload that is thrown at me daily. It's as if each item out of place is a tiny spark of distraction, pulling my attention away from where I need it to be. By keeping my space organised, I minimise these distractions, which helps me to focus better and feel more at ease.

As well as helping me concentrate, keeping order significantly cuts down on the mental energy I use making decisions. With ADHD, every decision can feel exhausting, like choosing where to put a misplaced item or figuring out what needs cleaning. When everything has a designated spot, the decision is made for me, freeing up precious cognitive resources for more demanding tasks. This organisation isn't just about being tidy; it's a strategy to keep my day running smoothly.

Having a neat and organised home also gives me a sense of control in the unpredictable sphere of ADHD. In a world where my attention and thoughts can feel hijacked by my brain's impulses, controlling my environment gives me back some of that power. It's my way of creating predictability and stability, not just for me but for my family.

Sometimes my need for order turns into a hyperfocus zone. I dive deep into organising a cupboard or planning the week's meals with an intensity that might seem peculiar to others. But in these moments of deep concentration, I feel a sense of accomplishment that ADHD often makes elusive.

And then there's the sensory aspect. I've noticed I'm more sensitive to my surroundings than most. A cluttered room feels chaotic, not just visually but deep in my core, adding to my sensory overload. A tidy space, in contrast, feels calming, almost like a physical manifestation of the quiet I desperately look for within my mind.

Explaining this need for organisation to my husband and daughters has been crucial. It's not just about liking things clean or being particular; it's about managing my ADHD and keeping my head above water. I want my home to be a place where my mind can rest and thrive among the beautiful chaos of our family life.

As I work through my journey with ADHD, I am in the continuous process of discovering how to best use this superpower. It is a path of self-discovery and adaptation, about what it means to be intelligent and capable in a world that is slow to recognise the value of neurodiversity.

*

Conversations with Eve and one of my closest friends, Lizzie, who also has ADHD, consist of an array of topics. We jump from one to the other with ease and have the ability to understand and keep up with the conversation. It's something that needs to be seen and heard to be believed. Our lives are made up of an abundance of what we call 'Side Quests'. These are the moments when we veer off our original conversation or task at hand to engage another without warning. At this point we yell or say, 'Side Quest!' We embrace our zigzag thought processes and actions.

Another one of my closest friends, Tahlia, also has the grand pleasure of being a part of these conversations. Despite not sharing our ADHD, she's gotten the hang of our rapid topic shifts, treating it like a spectator sport where the rules constantly change. She's become quite the expert at nodding along and jumping in where she can, a true friend who knows that when it comes to keeping up with us, it's best to just enjoy the ride.

I've discovered some things on my journey that I hadn't realised before. One is that I constantly interrupt people while they're speaking. I didn't notice how much I did this until I found out it was an ADHD trait. So if I ever do this to you, I'm not being rude and I'm not disinterested in what you have to say, it's just my way of relating and showing I understand. Or I have something to say and if I don't say it now, it may be lost in the land of random thoughts forever, never to be heard of again.

I've also discovered that not everyone has a constant narrator in their head, a very active internal monologue that can be incredibly distracting. Listening to some form of music while working helps me 'drown out' or regulate this internal chatter, allowing me to focus on my tasks.

My brain, it seems, is set to a different frequency than the rest – tuned into the secret language of broken toys and temperamental appliances. Where others see a mess, I see a puzzle waiting to be solved, my mind whirring into action like a detective piecing together clues at a crime scene. There's Sam, wielding tools with the subtlety of a bull in a china shop, while I'm there, the calm in the storm, saying, 'Hold up, let's think this through.' It's the classic clash of brute force meets brainpower, where I emerge as the unlikely handyman – or should I say, handyperson – of the household. This knack, this mechanical empathy, I owe to my dad, the real-life MacGyver. In the face of Armageddon, he's your guy, turning scraps into salvation. Growing up, I was his shadow, marvelling at how he could breathe life into the lifeless, a skill I've proudly inherited.

Now, for the science behind this mechanical wizardry: it's all about spatial intelligence and problem-solving prowess, two areas where my brain lights up like a Christmas tree. This ability to visualise the mechanics and internal workings of objects, to intuitively understand how things fit together and function, isn't just handy; it's a testament to a brain that's wired for innovative thinking and creative problem-solving. Neurologically speaking, it's a dance of neural networks, with my executive functions choreographing moves that combine attention to detail, working memory and cognitive flexibility in a way that sees solutions where others see dead ends. So, while Sam might go for the hammer, I'm aligning my neurons, plotting a course through the chaos with surgical precision. It's a beautiful mind at work, folks – just don't ask me to find my keys.

*

As parents, I believe it's essential to shift our focus from an obsession with grades to nurturing our children's passions. Not every child will shine in traditional subjects like English and maths; some will find their calling in dance, art or other creative fields. There's wisdom in the idea that if a child struggles with science but has a deep passion for art the answer isn't a science tutor – it's more art lessons. Our aim should be to encourage our children's natural inclinations and interests rather than squeezing them into a one-size-fits-all educational mould.

The reality is that the current educational system doesn't accommodate the diverse ways in which individuals think and learn. In my experience it can be not only frustrating but also disheartening because we don't fit the conventional academic mould. Recognising and valuing our unique talents and interests can empower us to pursue paths that bring joy and fulfilment, rather than pushing towards a standard of success that may not be in line with our true selves.

When it comes to navigating ADHD, I'm all about highlighting the silver linings for Eve. She's a master of creativity and uniqueness – not one to merely colour between the lines. She has a remarkable knack for diving deep into her interests, turning what she touches into something amazing. She's assembled all our prams effortlessly, sidestepping the instructions as if she has an intuitive map in her mind, guiding her on where each piece snaps into place. It's as if she approaches life like a grand, intricate puzzle, instinctively knowing where every piece belongs.

Whenever there's something to be built or fixed, we turn to Eve to sprinkle her magic. Tasks that might take Sam hours are wrapped up by Eve in no time. The way her mind whirls and weaves together solutions is nothing short of incredible. Her ability to look at an object or scene and take a picture within seconds that is on the same level of those taken by world-renowned photographers is mind-blowing.

Eve's journey isn't about sticking to the beaten path; it's about carving her own, using her talents and perspectives. In a world that often walks in straight lines, Eve dances to the rhythm of her own beat, and that's her greatest strength.

CHAPTER 14

ON BEING IN BUSINESS

I never imagined that one day I would become my own brand and business. In fact, even saying that sounds ridiculous. A decade ago such a career path was beyond my contemplation; it simply wasn't even on my radar. But life has a way of guiding us through unforeseen paths, opening doors to opportunities we don't anticipate. These opportunities allowed me to partner with brands that I admire and resonate with and create things that I am proud of. I've been fortunate to use my creativity, engaging in projects that I am passionate about.

I promote products as part of my job, and I understand why this might seem like I'm 'just plugging products'. The truth is, this is how I earn my living. Aligning with brands and businesses I believe in. Just like anyone else, I have responsibilities and bills to pay. The nature of my work is public, and I understand that it opens me up to both praise and criticism. However, at the end of the day, my primary goal is to fulfil my professional duties, just as anyone would in their respective roles. We all have different jobs, but the commonality lies in our need to support ourselves and our families.

I'm also involved in the family businesses, 28 by Sam Wood and 28GO. When Sam and I first met, my knowledge of fitness and wellbeing, which was his area of expertise, was, let's say, average. Although I always tried to keep up a certain level of fitness, at times it seemed overwhelming because of time and logistics. My routine wouldn't only involve an attempted hour-long workout at the gym, but also the additional time spent driving there, searching for parking, making my way to the gym, then looking around, feeling completely intimidated by everything in front of me. I'd find an area to work out or a machine to use, then I'd stand there, staring at it, thinking, 'WTF do I do with this now!'

I'd struggle and end up wasting time trying to set the machines to my preferences, all while trying to look like I knew exactly what I was doing. It was painful to say the least. This meant I spent the majority of my session at the gym confused and pretending to be doing something. This was a one-and-a-half to two-hour commitment for often not much benefit. Juggling work, studies and caring for Eve left me with little time to spare, let alone two hours to walk around a gym trying to work out what to do. Despite my efforts to incorporate gym sessions in my schedule, my attempts were always short-lived and I'd eventually cancel my membership.

When the gym option proved to be unsuccessful, I tried my own home workouts. I bought some weights and put together a little routine. But this was also unsustainable because I didn't really know what types of exercises were best for me or the amount of repetitions and sets I should be doing. I needed a straightforward, time-efficient workout solution that didn't require me to think about these things.

Living with my parents around the time of *The Bachelor*, my diet consisted of our delicious family dinners, which were generally pretty healthy. Our meals were never complete without a loaf of bread, which I could effortlessly consume entirely. I was aware that eating so much bread might not be great for my health, but it gave me so much pleasure! My main challenge was understanding portion control and the types of food I should be eating to reach my personal fitness goals as well as identifying possible alternatives. But my schedule was so packed that even thinking about dietary changes seemed overwhelming.

As a single mother attempting to balance my many responsibilities, all the while trying to make time for my health and fitness, I needed to do something that could seamlessly integrate into my lifestyle without requiring a two-hour daily commitment. Sam had already recognised this specific need for busy mothers and busy men and women in general – people who were looking to maintain both their mental and physical health – and needed a solution that was quick, easily accessible and didn't require a visit to the gym. The program had to feel approachable and convenient. Sam's strong understanding of this and, of course, extensive fitness and business experience led to the creation of 28 by Sam Wood.

From the start of Sam's business idea, I played a role in its development, as a guinea pig for his concepts. He would present new ideas, and I would evaluate their effectiveness and provide feedback, essentially acting as a real-world tester for the program. This collaborative work was crucial in the early stages, where much of the program's foundation was laid.

Our partnership was multifaceted; not only were we exploring a romantic relationship, but we were also creating what would become the 28 by Sam Wood business. This dynamic was unique – Sam, with his fitness expertise, and I, representing the target audience, made for an ideal team.

The 28 by Sam Wood program has continued to adapt and grow over time. Having three more children since the program began has enhanced Sam's already extensive understanding of women's health needs, particularly the physical changes associated with pregnancy and postpartum recovery. This personal experience strengthened his appreciation for the challenges and requirements in women's fitness, further tailoring the program to meet people's individual and evolving needs. To think that over 1 million Australians have trained or cooked with us and done the program now is just incredible.

The 28 business has further expanded to include a range of protein supplements that are now in over 1300 supermarkets and pharmacies around Australia.

Again, just incredible! Sam is always working on something new and exciting, and there's always work to be done by both of us. I may not be in the boardroom too often, that doesn't mean I am not playing a crucial role behind the scenes with key decision-making. It's just that my boardroom is the kitchen and lounge area of our house scattered with toys, laundry baskets and the sounds of kids laughing, playing, yelling, fighting and then back to laughing. My influential conversations happen directly with the CEO and my husband (but he knows who the boss really is!).

Above all, though, my most fulfilling role is and always will be being a mother to my four incredible daughters. A role that doesn't get anywhere near the recognition it deserves. Unfortunately women's search for equality has also increased our responsibilities – as if we didn't have enough already. We now need to excel not just as mums, homemakers and partners, but also as career-orientated 'boss bitches'. Despite supporting women's achievements in the business realm, there's the feeling that simply being a mum is no longer seen as enough. Today's society seems to expect us to be supermums and career-driven women simultaneously.

When I wasn't working regularly during my pregnancies, at various times when I was faced with forms asking for my occupation, I've hesitated to write 'mum/ housewife/home duties', fearing it won't appear to be enough. How sad. Motherhood is *the* most challenging job. However, we exist in a time where this role alone is often seen as inadequate. The values of motherhood are sometimes eclipsed and we've unwittingly overlooked how awesome being a mum is, because we're so focused on nailing it at work.

CHAPTER 15

ON FINDING BALANCE (OR NOT)

Navigating motherhood often feels like you're the captain of a ship sailing through a turbulent sea, where your wants and needs are tossed overboard to lighten the load for your crew – your family. Sam now knows me in my most prominent role: Snezana the stay-at-home working mum. Every now and then, he catches glimpses of Snezana the individual, the other part of me, the person with her own quirks and desires. But let's be real, wading through the chaos of nappy changes, toddler tantrums and teenage outbursts means that for the past seven years, these glimpses are just that ... glimpses.

So, while the balance between Snezana the individual and Snezana the stay-at-home working mum might lean heavily towards the latter at the moment, those rare moments of rediscovery, even if they're short-lived, are like finding treasure among the wreckage. Yes, it's a juggle, a dance, a sometimes frightfully overwhelming experience, but it's also filled with moments of unspeakable joy and the most intense love, proving that even in the most chaotic of storms, there's beauty and strength to be found.

In today's world, raising kids is a whole different ball game, and Sam and I are right in the trenches with our four girls. Back in the 80s and 90s, when we were young, things were tough, but we learned to be tough too. We weren't over-sensitive about every little thing done and said. If we got knocked down, we dusted ourselves off, got back up and moved on. That's the kind of resilience we want to pass on to our daughters.

We're living in a time when everyone seems to be walking on eggshells, afraid of saying the wrong thing or hurting someone's feelings. While it's great that people are more aware and respectful of each other's emotions, we also believe it's important for our girls to know how to handle it when things don't go their way. Life isn't always going to be smooth sailing, and not everyone is going to be nice and like you. That's just how it is. We want to prepare our daughters for that reality, to be strong but also to know how to manage their emotions. We want them to know that not everyone will share the same views, and that's okay, they don't have to. We all just need to respect each other's views and move on.

Parenting is a tough gig but we're doing what we can to make sure our girls grow up the way we think is best. We want them to be ready for the real world, where they'll face challenges, where they might not be liked by everyone, and where they won't always win. It's all about learning from their experiences and growing stronger in spite of them. We want them to understand that it's okay to feel upset or disappointed, but it's also important to learn how to deal with those feelings and keep going. Having said that, this is not an easy feat, as being a parent your natural instinct is to protect them and wrap them in cotton wool so they never need go through the obstacles you did. This I'm guilty of.

Even with our strong commitment to teach our kids resilience the way we learned it in the 80s and 90s, I realise that we're navigating a completely different world with our daughters. As we all know, the landscape has shifted dramatically since my childhood and today's pressures of social media and the digital age present challenges we never had to face. It's a reality where likes, comments and online personas can hugely impact a young person's self-esteem and mental health. Our lives and the lives of our children are so closely tied to the digital world. Phones aren't just phones anymore; they're lifelines to friends, gateways to information and tools for navigating day-to-day life. Everything from boarding passes to bank accounts is at our fingertips. While we might reminisce about the days when we didn't need a phone to meet up with friends or find our way, the truth is that those days are gone. Our kids are growing up in a world where digital literacy is just as important as learning to ride a bike. Acknowledging this shift doesn't mean we abandon our principles of teaching resilience and emotional regulation. Instead, it means adapting these lessons to fit the world they now live in and their lives. As parents, we need to educate ourselves on the pressures and challenges our kids face online and understand the impact they can have on their wellbeing. It's about finding a balance between encouraging them to engage with the digital world in a healthy, positive way, and also knowing when to put the phone down and experience life beyond the screen, 'the real world' as we old folk like to call it. It's not always easy, but we're in this together. But that doesn't mean Sam and I see eye to eye on all the parenting decisions – far from it, to be honest.

When it comes to discipline, I'm a 'no dessert if you don't eat all your dinner' kind of mum. I look at their plates after what feels like 30 minutes, during which time they've only eaten a quarter of a spoon of mashed potato, carrying on the entire time like I was making them eat poison. I finally say to them, 'Okay, no dessert, but you can leave the table.'

But in the same scenario, when Sam looks at their plates, he is the kind of dad who says, 'You're not having dessert till there's nothing on the plate, and I mean nothing. If there's even a smudge of mash on the plate, then there is not only no dessert, but you're not leaving the table.'

We also have different approaches when it comes to teen discipline. I'm 'You're grounded for a week – you can have your phone but you need to hand it in at 9 pm', and Sam's more, 'You're grounded for three months – that means no phone the entire time and you can use the iPad and laptop for schoolwork till 10 pm, but then you hand them in.'

We're a work-in-progress in this area!

*

There's so much advice out there now telling us we need to strive for balance, but what does that mean? To me, finding the perfect balance doesn't simply mean splitting my time evenly between work and family. It's more about finding the right mix, like trying to keep your balance on a seesaw. Some days, I'm all about work deadlines and emails, and other times I'm immersed in mum mode, playing and reading stories, not giving a second glance at emails. It's not about achieving perfect balance every day, instead it's about figuring out what works best for me and my family at any given moment. Sometimes I might lean too much one way and not enough the other, but that's okay. This sounds simple enough, but the hardest part is accepting 'it's okay'. The real win is in knowing it's fine to not always get it right and understanding that both my family and my jobs are important parts of my life. It's all about giving myself a break and not being hard on myself, which I often am. I'm learning as I go, remembering that love and trying my best are what really counts.

One of these tough times was when I was pregnant with Harper. Suddenly, I had to stop my early morning workouts that I'd normally wake to do at 5 am, I couldn't do as much work around the house or my own work, and I couldn't spend as much time playing with the kids. I was used to being constantly on the go, so when I was doing the bare minimum in all aspects of my life it felt like I wasn't myself anymore. I felt guilty. I felt I was letting my family and myself down. I've always been the type to just get on with things and keep going. But during that time, even walking to school felt like a marathon. Beating myself up over it definitely didn't help. Of course I knew not all pregnancies were easy, but this was a whole new level of tough for me.

Looking back, I'm not sure how I kept pushing through. In hindsight my daily breakdowns actually helped in a weird way. They were my reset button. This period was rough, but it taught me a lot. I learned it's okay to say, 'No I can't', and cut myself some slack. I was doing the best I could, and that had to be enough.

Finding balance isn't just about juggling your to-do list. It's about being kind to yourself when you can't do it all. It's realising that your best is good enough, even when it feels like it's not. It's about trying to keep something that resembles steady, even when the wheels have fallen off.

You never really clock off from being a mum, whether you have one kid or four kids like me. Sure, you can find time to be your own person, even through the parenting chaos, but when each child has their own personal struggle, my attention has to be divided not three, not four, but effectively five ways (five because I can't forget that hubby needs some attention too!). You find yourself in the eye of the storm, thinking, 'Well, I'm in a bit of a pickle.' And when you don't have an extended family nearby to call in reinforcements, you're basically sailing solo through rough waters. But within the madness and rough waters, there's a strange beauty in the chaos.

Crack of dawn hits and it's go-time in our household. I'm on kid and lunchbox duty and thankfully Sam can drop the girls off to school most days, leaving me with Harper, my little sidekick. I turn into a domestic Flash, dodging the shoe minefield on the floor left by Sam and our girls. After transforming the living area back to a living area from a toy and shoe store, I attempt to answer emails. If I can get a whole three minutes of uninterrupted work, I'm basically a productivity guru. But, like clockwork, Harper, my adorable little toothless interruption smiles, deciding it's outdoor adventure time.

Park time is a cocktail of fun and guilt. There I am, phone in hand, sneaking peeks at emails and requests for me to send assets across urgently and looking at deadlines between glances at the kids, while secretly worrying other parents might see me as the Instagram-scrolling, child-ignoring type. Little do they know, I'm trying to meet deadlines between pushes on the swing. So, if I sneak in some email time while they conquer the playground, it's all in the name of juggling life's endless tasks.

As hard as it is trying to find time for myself when there's an avalanche of 'mum work' and 'work work' to do, I'm on a mission to reclaim 'me' time. Inspired by Sam, who masters the art of me-time relaxation without a care in the world, I decided to take a leaf out of his book. Why not lounge by the pool instead of tackling a mountain of laundry to put away or conquering email Everest, which currently sits in the thousands?

There was this one time, with Sam and the girls out, I faced a decision: laundry, work or leisure? Channelling my inner Sam, I chose leisure. And let me tell you, soaking up the sun alone without hearing, 'Mum, look at me! Look at me!' and me yelling, 'Girls, stop fighting, share!' felt like a revolutionary act, even if my overactive brain kept ticking. As tiring as it can sometimes get, I'm reminded that one day I'll long for those voices to be interrupting my every thought and move. There will come a time when the tables will turn and I'll be vying for their attention.

Lying there, soaking up the rays, was a battle against my 'doer' instincts. I lasted about two minutes before my internal alarm bells rang, demanding I find something productive to do. However, armed with magazines, a playlist and jumping in and out of the pool, then tidying up the pool toys, I did it! It was my version of 20 minutes relaxing by the pool. Relaxing is hard work.

So, I'm learning. Learning that the world won't implode if the laundry sits a bit longer or if the floors aren't spotless. It's about finding those moments to just be, even if it means wrestling with my own guilt and productivity demons. Here's to more sunny relaxation and less laundry.

I'm at a pivotal moment in my life. I find myself standing at a crossroads, this time one of ambition and affection, where the road to career goals intersects with my love for being a mum. I find myself attracted towards a sense of achievement. I want to embrace more work, scale new heights and chase broader horizons independently from my husband and our family business. I want to catch up on my career goals, which I've repeatedly put on pause because of the challenges of my pregnancies and juggling a family.

But while working towards my version of what I believe to be 'success', I remember my most cherished role – being a mum to my four precious daughters. It's my hardest role, yet the one that brings me so much joy and happiness.

My priorities now lie within the walls of my home with my girls and my husband. This is my sanctuary. I still love to work; it's a huge part of who I am. But I know I need to pour my energy into the things that really excite me and feel right in my heart. Those are the goals that count, the ones that'll make my own path more fulfilling.

Everywhere we turn, society's all about hustle, telling women to go for more, aim higher and never stop, and this is amazing. However, I've learned not to be just about the hustle. I do things if they excite me and ignite my passion. If I'm not sure about something, I ask myself if these opportunities are worth it if they mean missing out on the little, priceless moments of my four girls growing up. Do these achievements, even if the world thinks they're a big deal, really mean something special to *me*? Some do, yes, and I move forward with them. I don't move forward with others because they often end up serving as hollow trophies, showing what I missed instead of what I got out of it.

Thinking about this, things start to click for me. The measure of true success isn't about the quantity of achievements but in their quality and their alignment with what is genuinely important to me. It makes me stop and ask myself: Is this goal, this career or personal win, really something I'm truly passionate about or am I just trying to add another notch in my belt to keep up with today's expectation of what women should be doing? If it's just about notches and satisfying expectations, then maybe it's time to step back, reassess and make sure what I'm doing is what I truly want deep down. Because in the end, the most important achievements are those that are felt deeply in my heart, not just those recognised by others.

CHAPTER 16

ON CARING LESS AND LOVING MORE

Growing up in Perth, I loved the beach. I learned to respect the power of the ocean and felt the happiest and most safe standing close to the shoreline. Being unexpectedly thrown into the spotlight after *The Bachelor* was like being swept up by a powerful current in open water. At first, the rush was exciting, lifting me to new, unexpected heights and bringing joy to my life. After all, this is how I met my husband. He is my lighthouse, guiding me through the choppy waters. But with visibility came vulnerability, especially in the huge, unpredictable ocean that is the spotlight. With every wave of support and kindness that rolls through, there is a current of criticism and scrutiny dragging me out. Each negative comment threatening to pull me under, it challenges my ability to keep my head above water.

To get through this, I first needed to learn to ride the waves, to find balance among the swirling water and always keep the horizon in sight – remembering the joy and love that the spotlight has brought to me, the connection I have formed with my husband and growing our family from just three of us to our beautiful family of six. The opportunity of a different career path, one that I'd never thought about before, allows me greater flexibility and this remains a source of strength and stability. Just as important is learning to see the difference between constructive feedback that can help me grow and propel me forward and harmful currents of negativity, with the sole purpose of pulling me under. Finding a path that allows me to detour into calmer waters, such as taking breaks from social media to reconnect with myself and loved ones, is a much-needed reset. I've also come to understand that behind every keyboard warrior there's a human soul who struggles with their own demons. As hard as it may be at times, remembering to have empathy towards them is crucial to looking after myself.

Having family and friends who can support me is also important. I make sure that those in my inner circle are true friends and have my best interests at heart. For too long, I was the silent one, my voice lost among others' opinions. This silence was born from a deep-rooted shyness and a fear of judgement. Sure, it may have taken me a while, but now, at forty-three, I've finally found my voice, with its unique insights and truths.

In finding my voice, I've not only set boundaries and formed a circle of genuine friendships, but I have also ensured that my daughters are surrounded by women of substance. Women who show that while life might be full of challenges, it's the courage to continue, to face each day with determination, that defines us. These women in my circle prove that success does not come without struggle and sacrifice. We all face our fair share of challenging days – days of doubt, frustration and setbacks. However, what matters most is our resilience, how we rise after each fall. This resilience, this refusal to be defined by our struggles, is what I want to teach my girls and what I also want them to see in me.

Being blessed with the gift of four incredible daughters is something that fills my heart with endless joy. I've had many ask the question 'Are you going to try for a boy?', as if my life is somehow incomplete. And I answer without any hesitation a definitive 'Absolutely not.'

Being a mum to my four girls is a privilege; it's the part of my life I cherish the most and brings me the greatest joy. Sure, I might be just a little biased, but to me, our daughters are simply perfect, each with their own and very distinctive personality and style. I love them boundlessly for who they are. My heart is so full of love for them. They make me laugh, they fill our home with joy, and even when times get tough, I wouldn't have it any other way. They are my pride and joy, and every moment with them is a treasure.

Without a doubt, my children are what I'm most proud of. Giving birth to them and being their mother is by far my life greatest achievement. Of course, I feel pride about getting my degree, having businesses and somewhere to call home, but none of that compares to how important my family is to me.

Money comes and goes, businesses open and close, status levels rise and fall. None of that really matters. The only thing that's forever is the connection you have with your family and the memories you make together. To know that my girls are happy, healthy, growing and strong is the most fulfilling thing I can imagine.

I want to pass my knowledge and lessons learned in life to my daughters. When I was young, I was constantly told that I couldn't do things – because I was a woman, because I wasn't 'university material', because I was unmarried, because I was … Every time I was told I couldn't do something, I heard the same thing: 'You're not enough.' That message was drummed into me. I listened to what I was being told, and I became self-conscious and scared to step out of my comfort zone. I felt insignificant. I thought I couldn't have dreams because they weren't realistic, or they were too far out of reach or too much for someone like me. I was wrong.

If I could tell my younger self anything, I would tell her she can have dreams and they are never out of reach if that is what she truly wants. That's what I'm teaching my girls: you can do anything you want to do.

But it's up to them to take the first steps. Nothing's going to happen if you just sit on the sidelines, waiting for a sign. It's scary to jump in, I know. The idea of stepping out of your comfort zone? Terrifying. But that's exactly where life starts getting interesting. Don't sell yourself short. Trust in yourself a bit more.

*

I've learned to embrace my journey of self-discovery by approaching my fears with openness and curiosity. If you can allow yourself to embrace these emotions, to truly engage with the depths of your fear and every part of you responding to this challenge, there is an immense freedom that comes from overcoming these fears.

Question the roots of your fear, their significance to your inner self, and think how freeing it is to know that beyond this fear may lie the path to fulfilment you've been looking for.

It is in this challenge and realisation that we have the choice to ride the waves, feel the fear and do it anyway. I believe this is the true meaning of courage – to acknowledge our fears, to feel them fully, and still, to proceed in spite of them, pushing ourselves towards the dreams and the life that awaits on the other side of our fears. Life has taught me to embrace new and unknown paths I once feared; now, I'm happy to see where the tide takes me.

Don't settle for less. Back yourself in. Feel the fear and do it anyway.

CHILDHOOD AND FAMILY PHOTOGRAPHS

Chapter 1
Top left: My mum with her parents and siblings, North Macedonia. Top row, from left: my baba Neda, tetka (aunty) Jonka, tetka Krstana and my dedo Milan. Bottom row, from left: my vuyće (uncle) Naum as a toddler, tetka Razmenka and my mum, Menka.
Top right: My mum, in her early twenties.
Bottom left: Curled up on the couch with my baba Neda in North Macedonia on a visit in 2004.
Bottom right: My dad with his parents and sister. From left: my baba Nika, my dad Marko, dedo Trifun and tetka Menka.

Chapter 2
Top: With my big sister, Lidija, Perth, 1982.
Second from top: With my big sister, Macedonia, 1984.
Second from bottom: With my siblings in Macedonia in my teens.
Bottom: Me, baby brother, Robert, and Lidija, 1988.

Chapter 3
Top left: Pregnant with Eve.
Top right: My squishy little Monkey.
Bottom left. Eve and my dad, working away in the backyard.
Bottom right: With my slightly bigger little Monkey.

Chapter 4
Top left: Slumped at the table at 4 am during a long night of study.
Top right: At the Eiffel Tower on our wonderful trip to Paris.
Bottom left: The Louvre.
Bottom right: Paris Disneyland.

Chapter 5
Top left: Mum giving Eve a horsey ride in the backyard.
Top right: This is about the time Eve started encouraging me to get out more.
Bottom: Eve and Mum at the family hobby farm.

Chapter 6
Top: Mother–daughter sleepover during home visits on *The Bachelor*.
Middle: One of the lovely *Bachelor* producers, Millie, during home visits.
Bottom: Sam and I.

Chapter 7
Top left and right: With my sister, Lidija, and brother, Robert, in Perth after *The Bachelor*.
Middle: Engaged!
Bottom: Minutes after we got engaged. A joyful selfie with Sam and Eve overlooking Wineglass Bay, Tasmania.

Chapter 8
Top left: With Sam, in Perth.
Top right: Sam and I just after our move to Melbourne.
Bottom: Sam and I at our family hobby farm in Perth – healing.

Chapter 9
Top left: With Sam in North Macedonia, 2018.
Top right: With Eve, photoshoot during my pregnancy with Willow.
Bottom left: Sam with Willow hours after I gave birth.
Bottom right: Beautiful Willow.

Chapter 10
Top: With my family on our wedding day. What a joyous day.
Middle left: Special moments at our engagement party as a family of three.
Middle left: Just married!
Bottom: Our little surprise wedding present, gorgeous Charlie.

Chapter 11
Top: Selfie with Dedo, Eve and Baba.
Bottom left: Eve with her beloved great-dedo and baba in their kitchen in Perth.

Bottom right: Eve and Willow with their great-baba Neda in North Macedonia.

Chapter 12
Top left: With Sam and Harper, just after her birth.
Top right: In hospital with Harper holding my finger.
Bottom left: In the ICU of another hospital, desperate to get to my baby.
Bottom right: Reunited with Harper for the first time since her birth.

Chapter 13
Top left: Me in North Macedonia; if only I'd known then why my mind worked the way it does.
Top right: With Eve standing on top of Samuel's Fortress, North Macedonia, 2018. Two peas in a pod, in more ways than one.
Bottom left and right: With Eve, being our glorious selves.

Chapter 14
Top left: 28 work work work work.
Top right: In my office at 28 headquarters.
Bottom: The family did daily workouts during Covid.

Chapter 15
Top: Sam, my brother Rob, Eve and my nieces Elle and Ava at the family hobby farm.
Bottom left: With my beautiful girls, 2023. Clockwise from left: Eve, Harper, Willow and Charlie.
Bottom right: Easter fun – the girls with their cousins. Front row from left: Charlie, Harper, Kleo, Willow. Back row from left: Elle, Eve and Ava.

Chapter 16
The Wood family!

hachette
AUSTRALIA

If you would like to find out more about
Hachette Australia, our authors, upcoming events
and new releases you can visit our website or our
social media channels:

hachette.com.au
 HachetteAustralia
  HachetteAus